East Riding Chapels and Meeting Houses

by

DAVID AND SUSAN NEAVE

EAST YORKSHIRE LOCAL HISTORY SOCIETY

1990

Nonconformist chapels dominate many East Riding village streets, as did the Primitive Methodist chapel, Ratten Row, North Newbald. Built 1878, architect William, Freeman. Demolished 1987 (Postcard C. Ketchell)

CHAPELS IN THE LANDSCAPE

Simple former Primitive Methodist chapel of 1870 at Moortown, Brandesburton, which stands isolated over two miles from the nearest settlement.

© East Yorkshire Local History Society 1990

ISBN 900349.44.1

Printed by Clifford Ward & Co. (Bridlington) Ltd.

PREFACE

Although rightly famed for its fine medieval and Victorian Anglican churches, East Yorkshire was in the early 20th century predominantly a region of rural Methodist chapels. Many settlements had two, Wesleyan and Primitive, and the village without any at all was very rare indeed. In the area of the former administrative county of the East Riding, that is excluding Hull, over 600 nonconformist chapels, some 530 of which were Methodist, were built between the late 17th century and the outbreak of the First World War. This booklet has been produced to celebrate this important aspect of the history of East Yorkshire and to draw attention to the great need to preserve the best examples of buildings that have for far too long been under appreciated. In the last twenty-five years many chapels have closed and although a large number have found new uses a high proportion have been demolished or rendered unrecognisable by unsympathetic conversion. The gazetteer appended to this booklet has had to frequently be amended when yet another chapel closure or demolition was reported.

This publication had its origins in work carried out by a Nonconformist Buildings Recording Group established in 1976 by the East Yorkshire Local History Society under the leadership of David Neave and Olga Reckitt. The group whose active members included Mr. W. F. Atkinson, Miss I. Cooper, Mr. E. Fryer, Mrs. J. Henley, Miss D. King, Mrs. O. Reckitt, and Mr. R. E. and Mrs. R. Thistleton, had carried out a survey of part of the East Riding by 1980. The survey was thereafter undertaken by David and Susan Neave, with some assistance from Margaret Bryan, and completed in 1989, an appropriate date, it being 300 years since the passing of the Toleration Act which provided for the licensing of dissenting meeting-houses and led to a great upsurge of chapel building, and 250 years since the laying of the foundation stone of the first Methodist building, the New Room, Bristol, in May 1739.

In all some 350 chapels or former chapels have been photographed and brief notes made on duplicated forms. These will eventually be deposited in Humberside County Archives Office. Updating of the work has been generally carried out except in the case of south Holderness, which was surveyed very fully by Mr. and Mrs. Thistleton in 1978-80. The Thistletons' work is a model of how to carry out a survey, with excellent photographs, plans and a wealth of additional information. They chased up material on every known chapel, whether in use, converted or demolished, and from local informants pieced together a full account of the chapel's history and internal arrangements. It is sad to record that Mr. Thistleton died in 1988.

We dedicate this study to Olga Reckitt, who has provided us with support and inspiration over many years.

David and Susan Neave
Centre for Regional and Local History
University of Hull   December 1989

NONCONFORMITY AND CHAPEL BUILDING IN THE EAST RIDING

INTRODUCTION

Despite a strong Puritan tradition, and initial enthusiasm for the Society of Friends and other dissenting groups in the mid 17th century, there was little support for nonconformity in the East Riding by the mid 18th century. In 1743 only 11 dissenting meeting houses were recorded in the riding (7 Presbyterian or Independent, 3 Quaker and one Baptist). The situation was very different at the time of the Religious Census of 1851, when there were at least 390 licensed nonconformist meeting places (350 Methodist, 26 Independent or Congregational, 10 Baptist, 2 Quaker, and one each for the Unitarians and Latter Day Saints). Taking into account the percentage share of total attendances at places of worship on 31 March 1851 the East Riding, including Hull, was the fourth most dissenting 'county' in England, and second only to Cornwall in percentage of attendances at Methodist chapels. In some of the riding's registration districts, particularly Pocklington, Howden and Driffield, the Methodist share was exceptionally high. In the Driffield district the attendances were: Anglican 3,646 (31%), Methodist 7,057 (60.5%) and other dissent 987 (8.5%)

In 1865 the incumbent of Acklam reported to the archbishop of York that out of a population of about 800 'I should think there are not 20 real churchmen ... I believe that almost every individual in the parish leans to and supports dissent'. Other incumbents gave similar reports: at Broomfleet 400 out of a population of 500 were dissenters, at Bempton four-fifths of the people were Methodists, and the estate village of Burton Agnes was said to be almost entirely Wesleyan. In 1894 it was stated that every farmer but one in Sledmere was a Methodist and that there was not a real churchman among the whole population at Lund. By the end of the 19th century the quantity and scale of nonconformist chapels provided a visual confirmation of the strength of dissent in the East Riding.

Number of chapels built or rebuilt in the East Riding, 1770-1919

	Wesleyan	Primitive	Other	Total
1770-9	2	-	1	3
1780-9	10	-	1	11
1790-9	14	-	1	15
1800-9	29	-	10	39
1810-19	47	1	9	57
1820-9	40	34	6	80
1830-9	33	33	4	70
1840-9	27	24	3	54
1850-9	15	20	3	38
1860-9	21	42	6	69
1870-9	22	31	11	64
1880-9	13	9	3	25
1890-9	16	7	0	23
1900-9	15	5	4	24
1910-19	2	4	1	7
Total	306	210	63	579

Chapels were built in 241 settlements in the East Riding, of which 115 had both Wesleyan and Primitive chapels, 91 solely a Wesleyan chapel and 31 solely a Primitive chapel. Twenty-six (13.5%) of the 192 parishes in the East Riding had no nonconformist chapel by the end of the 19th century, and of these only five had more than 200 inhabitants in 1851 (Birdsall, Kirby Underdale, Everingham, Londesborough and Wressle). All five were 'closed' parishes under the control of a single or one major landowner, who seemingly actively discouraged the building of a chapel. There were also no chapels in the 'closed' settlements of Boynton, Brantingham, Burnby, Howsham, Leconfield, Scampston, Rise, Routh and

Winestead and, more surprisingly, in the much larger estate village of Escrick, which had a population of 700 and a Liberal landlord, Lord Wenlock, who provided allotments, a co-operative store and a friendly society for the community. At Warter the Primitive Methodists found it impossible in the 1860s to acquire land on which to build a chapel, and were prevented from obtaining any sort of building in which to hold services, because of the opposition of Lord Muncaster. Other landlords provided sites for chapels. The Boyntons gave land for Wesleyan chapels at Burton Agnes (1837) and Barmston (1839) and leased a site for a Primitive chapel at Haisthorpe (1888). Sir Tatton Sykes, a great builder of Anglican churches, granted land for Primitive chapels at Wansford (1864), Wetwang (1870) and Sledmere (1889). The last was given in the face of determined opposition by the Anglican incumbent.

The two great boom periods of chapel building were the 1820s and 1830s and the 1860s and 1870s. Reverses in the late 1840s and 1850s and from the late 1870s coincide with periods of agricultural depression and hardship. In 1886 the *Primitive Methodist Magazine* noted: 'There has been little more activity in the work of chapel and school extension, as the times are not favourable to this kind of effort in our community, since we have to depend mainly on the wage-earning class, and they have sorely felt the pinch of straitened circumstances lately'.

The extent of rural chapel building is remarkable when one considers that the congregations were largely drawn from the poorer section of the community. There were a few wealthy benefactors such as the Bells of Portington Grange, for the Wesleyans, or the Hodges of Hull, for Primitive Methodists, but generally, as the rector of Catwick remarked in 1865, the Primitive Methodists came from the labouring class and the Wesleyans from 'the class just above them such as the village shop keeper, blacksmiths, or smaller tenant of land'. It was these people who had to raise the funds for chapel building.

The money spent on chapel building rose steadily throughout the 19th century. Information on 85 East Riding village chapels built during the years 1820-1909 shows that the average spent on each chapel was £111 in 1820-39, £156 in 1840-59, £375 in 1860-79, and £731 in 1880-1909. In the 1820s and 1830s a number of chapels were built for less than £100, for example Wilberfoss Primitive chapel, which cost only £63 in 1824. As chapels became larger and grander in the 1840s and 1850s costs rose but even so the Primitive chapel at Atwick cost only £90 in 1856, in contrast to the £460 spent on Nafferton Primitive chapel two years later.

In the later 19th century, when Methodism was clearly the dominant force in the religious life of the East Riding, both Wesleyans and Primitives were prepared to spend large sums to show it. Over £800 was spent on North Cave Primitive chapel in 1870 and Langtoft Wesleyan chapel cost £1,000 in 1876. The greatest spending was, however, in the towns, where the sects vied with each other to erect the largest and most lavish building. At Great Driffield the Congregational church built in 1866 cost £3,000, the Primitive chapel of 1876 cost over £5,000, and the Wesleyan chapel of 1880 cost over £7,000. Immense sums were spent on new chapels in Bridlington. On St. John Street the Primitive chapel, erected in 1877, cost £3,085, and the Wesleyan chapel of 1884 cost £4,440, while at the Quay the United Methodist Free Church chapel of 1872 cost £3,000, the massive Wesleyan chapel of 1873 about £7,500, the Primitive Methodist chapel of 1878, £3,486, and the Congregational chapel of 1879 nearly £4,000. By the early 20th century village chapels were costing over £1,000. The Wesleyan chapel of 1903 at Bempton cost £1,050 and that of 1907 at Kilham £1,200.

Where did the money come from to finance chapel building on this scale? Considerable amounts came through voluntary subscriptions but often, far too often, the bulk of the cost was met through loans. Few chapels were opened 'debtless', as happened with Watton

Primitive chapel in 1887. The *Primitive Methodist Magazine* noted in 1863 that West Lutton chapel had cost 'six hundred pounds, three hundred pounds of which have been obtained or promised by means of a bazaar, tea meetings, donations, and the opening services. The remaining three hundred pounds have been borrowed on note at four per cent'. In 1878-9 the Wesleyans at Bridlington Quay borrowed a total of £3,084 12s. 9d. at four or four and a half per cent from 10 individuals and a bank.

It was not unusual for chapel debts to remain for many years. In 1857 it was said of Howden Primitive chapel that it 'was one of those very unhappy cases of chapel building where feelings were allowed to exercise more influence than judgement; hence for years it has been burdened'. Weaverthorpe Primitive chapel had a debt of £160 on it when opened in 1841 and had reduced it by only £40 some 20 years later. 'The sum for a society consisisting of five members, with a small congregation, was found to be a heavy burden'. In the late 1880s it was calculated that the 70 Primitive Methodist chapels on the Wolds had cost £39,943 to build and still had £15,005 to pay off.

The need to pay off chapel debts led to heightened activity on the part of the congregations. Money was raised by religious and social events and the sale of seats. Although opponents accused the chapels of using teas, treats, entertainments, bazaars, and the 'frequent introduction of female preachers and other exciting means' to increase membership, it was just such events that contributed to the vital role that chapels played in village life.

EAST RIDING NONCONFORMITY

Owstwick Quaker Meeting House built c.1670 Demolished.

17th-century Quaker gravestones, Hornsea. These stones mark the graves of members of the Acklam family. There are many such burial sites in the East Riding but few with gravestones.

QUAKERS

The Society of Friends (Quakers) found many supporters in the East Riding following a visit by George Fox to Yorkshire in the winter of 1651-2. By the early 1660s weekly meetings were being held in villages throughout Holderness, the Vale of York and the Wolds. Membership declined sharply after 1720.

Thirteen East Riding settlements had Quaker meeting houses before 1914: Bridlington (1678, replaced 1810 and 1903), North Cave (1687, rebuilt 1793) Owstwick (c. 1670), Skipsea and Elloughton (late 17th century), Beverley (1702, replaced 1714 and 1810), Hutton Cranswick (1706-7), Barmby Moor (1707), Hornsea (by 1711, replaced 1750), Welwick (1718), East Cottingwith (1788), Knapton (by 1815), and Bubwith (1879).

Quaker Cottage, Hornsea. Formerly used as a meeting house, it was given to the Quakers by Peter Acklam in 1750.

Bridlington Baptist chapel, Applegarth Lane, 1699.
The oldest and smallest nonconformist meeting house in East Yorkshire.

Hedon Particular Baptist chapel, Magdalen Gate, 1801.
Closed c.1910

BAPTISTS

The first recorded Baptist congregation in the East Riding was established at Bridlington in 1698. A minuscule meeting house, which still survives, was built the following year. This was replaced by a new chapel in 1713. The sect spread only slowly through the area during the next century, with chapels being built at Bishop Burton in 1770 and Driffield in 1788. The general religious revival in the early 19th century affected the Baptists and the following chapels were built or rebuilt: Hedon (1801), Beverley (Scotch Baptist 1808, replaced 1888), Hunmanby (1816), Skidby (1819), Kilham (1819), Nafferton (with Independents 1821), Preston (1828), Beverley (Particular Baptist 1834, rebuilt 1910), Hutton Cranswick (1841, rebuilt 1880), Driffield (1861), North Newbald (1867 and 1874), Woodmansey (1872), and Bridlington (1874).

Great Driffield Baptist chapel, King Street, 1788.
Closed 1861. One of the few chapels with a burial ground.

INDEPENDENTS, PRESBYTERIANS AND CONGREGATIONALISTS

The older Congregational churches traditionally trace their origins directly to Independent or Presbyterian congregations associated with Puritan ministers who were ejected from the Anglican church in 1662. There is, however, no evidence for a purpose-built meeting house existing in the East Riding before the 1690s. The earliest Independent (I) or Presbyterian (P) meeting houses were built to the west of Hull, at Swanland (I 1693), Cottingham (P by 1697), and South Cave (I 1718), and in the towns of Beverley (P by 1694), Bridlington (P 1698), and Howden (I 1722). In the early 18th century there were said to be congregations of 450 at Beverley and 800 at Cottingham and Swanland combined.

It was not until the early 19th century that there was a further spate of Independent chapel building, with new congregations established at Great Driffield (1802), Pocklington (1807), Market Weighton (1809), Elloughton (1814), Muston (1815), Bridlington Quay (1817), and Rillington (1818). In Holderness the home mission of Fish Street chapel, Hull, was responsible for chapels being built at Skipsea (1801), Patrington (1802), Long Riston (1803), Hornsea (1808), Leven (1809), Brandesburton (1809), Beeford (1810), Foston (1814), and North Frodingham (1820). Independent or Congregational chapels have existed in 28 East Riding settlements.

Swanland URC (Congregational) church, 1803.
Replaced meeting house of 1693. Schoolrooms added 1877.

Cottingham: Zion URC (Congregational church, Hallgate, 1819.
Architect Appleton Bennison of Hull

EARLY METHODISM

Methodism reached York by 1743 and Hull by 1746. From these two centres the movement spread rapidly through the East Riding, assisted no doubt by the 20 visits John Wesley made to the area between 1752 and his death in 1791. By 1764 there were at least 21 licensed Methodist meeting houses in the East Riding, none of them purpose built, the majority being private houses or converted barns.

Dissenting meeting house certificates provide the first evidence of chapel building, commencing with the meeting house erected at Bridlington in 1775. This was registered in 1777, along with a 'new preaching house' at Great Driffield. By 1800 a further 14 purpose-built meeting houses had been registered: Beverley, Wood Lane (registered 1782,) Market Weighton (1786), Holme on Spalding Moor (1787), Garton on the Wolds (1788), Howden (1788), Kilham (1789), Newport (1789), Acklam (1790), Westow (1793), East Heslerton (1794), Weaverthorpe (1794), Pocklington (1795), Riccall (1798), and Flamborough (1799). There are also pre-1800 Methodist chapels still existing at East Cottingwith (1796) and Uncleby (1796).

The early Market Weighton chapel is of particular importance, for John Wesley preached there in 1787. The recent restoration of the building by Market Weighton Civic Trust is to be highly commended.

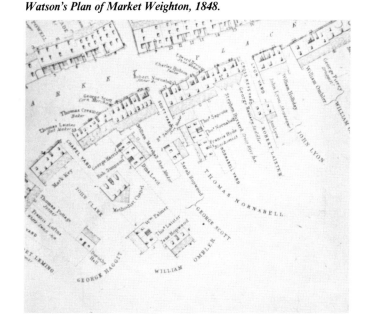

Market Weighton. Top: the oldest surviving Methodist chapel in the East Riding. Built 1786.
Bottom: the chapel was built in a yard off Market Place. From **William Watson's Plan of Market Weighton, 1848.**

Ganton. Cottage converted to Wesleyan chapel in the 19th century.

Sancton. Wesleyan chapel built in 1815 in the garden of the family home of Thomas Jackson, future President of the Wesleyan Methodist Conference.

Knapton. Wesleyan Chapel. Converted from a barn for joint use by Methodists and Quakers in 1815.

Newport. Original first-floor Wesleyan chapel, built in 1789 with houses/shops on ground floor.

Early preachers' plan for Hull Primitive Methodist Circuit Aug.-Oct. 1819.

North Cave *Primitive Methodist chapel. Opened 26 July 1819 it was the first Primitive chapel built north of the Humber. Demolished.*

PRIMITIVE METHODISM

Primitive Methodism which had spread steadily up the Trent valley since its establishment in 1811 reached the East Riding in January 1819. The co-founder of the sect, William Clowes, arrived at Hull on 15 January. He had been preceded a few days earlier by Miss Jane Brown, a pioneer Primitive Methodist preacher. Clowes's journal recounts his active missioning of the villages around Hull during the following few months. He and his fellow preachers, including 'Praying Johnny' Oxtoby of Warter, had great success and chapels were soon being built. The first was at North Cave in 1819, followed by others at Pocklington (1820), Acklam, Flamborough, Flixton, Great Driffield, Leavening, Melbourne, Middleton, North Duffield, Seaton Ross, and Skirlaugh (all 1821). Before long many East Riding villages had both Wesleyan and Primitive Methodist chapels.

Muston Primitive Methodist chapel, 1824.

Great Hatfield *Primitive Methodist chapel, 1862. Enlarged 1901.*

Beverley *Primitive Methodist chapel, Wednesday Market, built 1825. Replaced 1867.*

Dunswell Methodist New Connexion chapel, 1817. Closed 1968.

Great Driffield United Free Methodist Church chapel, Bridge Street, 1863. Architect Charles E. Taylor.

OTHER SECTS

Other than Primitive Methodism, the various Methodist splinter groups had little success in the East Riding. Methodist New Connexion chapels are recorded at Dunswell (1817) and Meaux (by 1851). Both the Independent Methodists (1847) and the Wesleyan Methodist Association (1830s) had chapels at Heslington and the short-lived body of Church Methodists built chapels in 1825 at Beverley, Cherry Burton and Woodmansey. Wesleyan Reformers and their successor body, after 1857, the United Methodist Free Church opened chapels at Ellerker (1850), Bridlington (1852), Beverley (1856), Great Driffield (1863), Hessle (1863), and Burythorpe (1865). By the end of the century the Salvation Army had citadels at Beverley (1885-6), Cottingham (1888), and Norton. The Inghamites, followers of the 18th century West Riding evangelist the Revd. Benjamin Ingham, built their only East Riding chapel at Howden (1820).

Beverley Salvation Army Citadel, Wilbert Lane, 1885-6. Architect E. J. Sherwood, London. Demolished 1988.

CHAPEL ARCHITECTURE

The first indoor meetings of dissenting groups were held in private houses or outbuildings. Henry Woodcock, in *Piety amongst the Peasantry: Being Sketches of Primitive Methodism on the Yorkshire Wolds*, recalls that at Middleton on the Wolds the preaching place was 'a stable-like structure past a wheelwright's shop, up an uninviting back yard', and at Little Driffield the meeting room was in a stable that retained its crib and a manure heap by the entrance. In summer the stench was unbearable and Woodcock notes; 'We preached some of our shortest sermons in that sanctuary'. A not untypical succession of meeting places is recalled for Cranswick, where the Primitive Methodists began with open-air services on the green and then moved to a cart-shed. They next progressed to a 'barn-like place' in Dove's Court. 'Its acoustic properties were bad, and tins of all sorts and sizes were suspended from the ceiling to air the sound of the preacher's voice'. They afterwards removed to a small chapel in Norris's yard before making their final home in a much larger Italianate chapel, overlooking the green, built at a cost of £700 in 1864.

This last building, in multi-coloured brick and slate, was architect-designed, unlike its predecessor, which would most probably have been erected in locally-produced bricks and pantiles by the village bricklayer with the help of the congregation.

The illustrations on the following pages, principally of Methodist chapels, have been chosen to show the progression of chapel building from the late 18th to the early 20th century. John Wesley directed in the 1770s that 'all preaching-houses be built plain and decent; but not more expensive than is absolutely necessary'. They were to have 'doors and windows enough' and the windows were to be 'sashes opening downward'. In the 1760s and 1770s Wesley promoted the building of octagonal chapels but none was built in the East Riding. Here the earliest chapels are rectangular and if the entrance is at the side they have a gabled or hipped roof. Single- and two-storey gable-entrance chapels might have a simple pediment, a feature that was enlarged upon in the 1830s and 1840s to produce a fuller Classical facade. From mid century, with the general use of professional architects, the 'battle of the styles' began. The first Gothic chapels appeared and they became more church-like as the century progressed. Supporters of the Gothic style saw it as the true Christian architecture, while opponents condemned it for its association with Roman Catholicism. The Classical style, which in turn was branded as pagan, took on an increasingly individualistic Italiante or Renaissance aspect which produced lavish facades in stone or polychrome materials. A free Gothic style, however, predominated for all sects by the early 20th century.

Market Weighton Methodist chapel, 1786. (Drawing by Eugene Fisk)

Newport Methodist chapel, 1814, with burial ground. (Drawing by Eugene Fisk)

EARLY CHAPELS

The two-storey square chapel with hipped pantiled roof is the most distinctive type of early Methodist building in the East Riding. Round-headed and pointed-arched openings are a feature of this style, which was in use from the 1780s to the 1820s. The best examples are at Market Weighton and Newport. The latter retains a fine interior.

Weaverthorpe Wesleyan Methodist chapel. Registered 1794, altered 1814.

Acklam Zion Primitive Methodist chapel, 1821. A late example of this style. See also Beverley Primitive chapel of 1825 (p.13 above).

East Cottingwith Wesleyan Methodist chapel, 1796. Bay to the left of door added 1868.

Bolton Wesleyan Methodist chapel, 1869. Architect Thomas Grant of Pocklington. Burial ground attached.

Acklam Wesleyan Methodist chapel, 1794. Now Anglican church.

Dunnington, Holderness, Wesleyan Methodist chapel, 1858.

The smaller village chapel from the late 18th century to the mid 19th century was usually a single storey rectangular structure with an entrance door, flanked by windows, in the middle of one of the long sides. Simple straight-headed sashes were eventually succeeded by round headed windows. The roof was either straight gabled or hipped.

Little Weighton Wesleyan Methodist chapel, 1827.

South Cave Wesleyan Methodist chapel, 1816. Closed 1943.

North Cave Centenary Wesleyan Methodist chapel, 1839.

Hessle Wesleyan Methodist chapel, 1813. Closed 1877.

The pedimented gable-ended chapel was an early alternative to the square hipped type, particularly for larger buildings. Good examples survive at Hornsea (1814), South Cave (1816), and Rillington (1818), all now disused.

CLASSICAL

Bishop Burton Wesleyan Methodist chapel, 1840.
(Drawing by Eugene Fisk)

The Classical chapels built in the East Riding in the 1830s and 1840s were attractive but modest and could not view with H. F. Lockwood's magnificent chapels in Great Thornton Street (1841) and Albion Street (1842), Hull, sadly both demolished.

Beverley Particular Baptist chapel, Well Lane, 1834. Demolished 1909.

Beverley Wesleyan Reform Methodist chapel, Trinity Lane, 1856. Now Masonic Hall.

Detail of Corinthian capital, Wesleyan Reform chapel, Beverley.

Sutton-on-Hull Wesleyan Methodist chapel, Church Street, 1859.

The former Wesleyan Reform chapel (later United Methodist Free Church) in Beverley has a fine Late Grecian facade with giant Corinthian pilasters and a pediment. This contrasts with the simpler pedimented facade of the Wesleyan chapel at Sutton, built three years later, which has a porch with Tuscan columns.

ITALIANATE

Nonconformist chapel architecture came into its own with the adoption of a free Italianate style in the 1860s. The buildings displayed on this and the following two pages could be nothing but chapels. The Market Weighton Wesleyan chapel, with its pilastered and arched facade and sides in white stock brick and Harehill stone, proudly fronts on to the main street, replacing the simple early building of 1786 which is out of sight in a yard to the left.

Cottingham *Wesleyan Methodist chapel, Hallgate, 1879. Architect William Ranger.*

Market Weighton *Wesleyan Methodist chapel, 1868. Architect William Botterill.*

Hutton Cranswick *Wesleyan Methodist chapel, 1861. Architect William Hawe.*

Great Driffield Wesleyan Methodist chapel, 1880.
Architect H. J. Paull. *(Postcard P. Thompson)*

Bridlington Quay Wesleyan Methodist chapel, 1873.
Architect William Botterill.

Beverley Wesleyan Methodist chapel, 1891.
Architects Morley & Woodhouse.

Bridlington: Burlington Wesleyan chapel, St. John Street, 1884. Architect Joseph Earnshaw.

Burton Fleming Wesleyan Methodist chapel, 1883.

Flamborough Wesleyan Methodist chapel, 1889. Architect Joseph Earnshaw. Demolished 1989.

For the most spectacular late Victorian Wesleyan chapels one has to go to the East Riding's largest towns, Bridlington, Beverley and Driffield. The vast chapels in the last two places are strangely tucked away, but that at Bridlington Quay, with its huge pilasters and French style turrets, dominates the street. Its rival the Burlington Wesleyan chapel, which has turrets with an Eastern flavour, is by the local architect Joseph Earnshaw, who elsewhere produced a distinctive series of chapels of polychrome bricks. (see back cover).

Ellerton Wesleyan Methodist chapel, 1811.

Heslington Wesleyan Methodist chapel, 1844.

Arched openings occur in the fine early chapels at Market Weighton, 1786, and Bubwith, 1796, (demolished). The former has inter-locking glazing bars a feature that has recently been re-introduced at Newport chapel, 1814. Gothic openings were particularly popular in the Vale of York in the second decade of the 19th century, e.g. Elvington, 1810, Melbourne 1811, and Ellerton 1811. A late example at Heslington 1844 has 'Tudor Gothic' windows at front and sides.

The choice of a more overt Gothicism for Burton Agnes Wesleyan chapel, 1837, was probably influenced by the donor of the site Sir Henry Boynton, the resident squire.

Wold Newton Wesleyan Methodist chapel, 1839.

Burton Agnes
Wesleyan Methodist chapel, 1837.

GOTHIC

Before the mid 19th century East Riding nonconformists built plainly and generally eschewed any extravagant detail or architectural style. An exception was the common use of arched openings and interlocking tracery in Methodist chapels from the earliest period. These 'Gothic' features were largely confined to Wesleyan chapels.

The first East Riding nonconformist chapel fully in Gothic style albeit in a debased form, was the Church Methodist chapel at Beverley, built in 1825. The pinnacled and castellated facade with a four-light interlocking traceried window flanked by lancets above arched entrances, was no doubt chosen to emphasise the wish of this short-lived breakaway Methodist sect to become an auxiliary branch of the Anglican church.

*Beverley Church Methodist chapel, Landress Lane, 1825.
Demolished c.1840.*

In 1850 a Wesleyan Methodist minister, Frederick J. Jobson, published with the support of the Wesleyan Chapel Committee a work entitled *Chapel and School Architecture*. Jobson, whose first appointment was to the Partington Wesleyan circuit, had been apprenticed to the Roman Catholic architect Edward James Willson of Lincoln. In his book he strongly advocated the use of the Gothic style, which he claimed was 'the most *appropriate* and the most *economical* style of chapel building'. For 'Gothic architecture is Christian architecture, as distinctly and emphatically, as the Egyptian, Greek and Roman are Pagan'. He suggested that it was often hard to tell a Roman or Greek style chapel from a concert room, a theatre or a town hall, yet a Gothic chapel was clearly a religious building. Jobson's views were highly influential during the second half of the 19th century.

*Village chapel from F. J. Jobson, **Chapel and School Architecture**, 1850*

Withernsea (Owthorne) *Wesleyan chapel, Cammidge Street, 1857. Demolished.*

Newland (Hull) *Wesleyan chapel, Newland Avenue, 1858. Architect William Botterill. Demolished.*

Brough *Wesleyan chapel, 1852.*

Sunk Island *Wesleyan chapel, 1858. Demolished c. 1968. (Photo. John Meadley)*

Norton *Wesleyan chapel, 1857. Architect William Lovel of Norton.*

A series of modest Gothic Wesleyan chapels were built in the East Riding following the publication of Jobson's book. The first was at Brough (1852), and others followed at Duggleby (1856), Norton, Naburn, Withernsea (all 1857), Sunk Island and Newland (both 1858); only the first three survive. All the architectural detail of Duggleby chapel has been destroyed; this is unfortunate for when it was opened its design was said to have been 'taken from Mr. Jobson's *Gothic Chapel Architecture*'.

North Duffield Wesleyan chapel, 1876

Elloughton Primitive Methodist chapel, 1866.

Nafferton Wesleyan chapel, 1907.

The early Gothic Methodist chapels were all Wesleyan, for the Primitives were less enthusiastic about a style closely associated with Roman Catholicism and the Anglican church. Gothic features, however, began to appear in Primitive chapels in the 1860s, but rarely is the detail elaborate. Elloughton Primitive chapel, built in 1866, has a facade dominated by a three-light window in the Early English style. This simple style was favoured by the Primitives and is used in the ambitious village chapel at Burstwick.

Village chapels, such as North Duffield Wesleyan, of 1876, might have no more Gothic detail than pinnacles and pointed-arched windows but in the towns nonconformists were erecting full-blown Gothic churches. At Hessle and Filey in 1876 the Wesleyans built impressive Gothic buildings with spire-bedecked corner towers. The spire on Hessle chapel seems to have been erected in rivalry to that on the medieval Anglican church nearby. Other nonconformist sects were happy to fully reproduce the plan and detail of medieval churches. Samuel Musgrave's Congregational church at Hornsea, of 1872, has transepts as well as tower and spire.

*Hornsea URC (Congregational) church, 1872
Architect Samuel Musgrave.*

*Hessle Wesleyan chapel, 1876.
Architect William Botterill.*

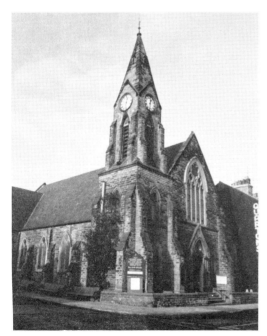

Filey Trinity Wesleyan chapel, 1876.

*Burstwick Primitive Methodist chapel, 1898.
Architect T. B. Thompson.*

Beverley *Particular Baptist chapel, Lord Roberts Road, 1910. Architect G. F. Pennington.*
(Drawing by Eugene Fisk)

In the early years of the 20th century a number of chapels were built in a free Gothic style. Notable examples include the now demolished Wesleyan chapel at Withernsea, of 1900, designed by Gelder and Kitchen, and two Primitive chapels at Keyingham and Hessle designed by T. B. Atkinson in 1909. Also attributable to Atkinson is the Primitive chapel at Welwick, with its dominant five-light Perpendicular style window. Undoubtedly the finest chapel in a free Gothic style is the former Baptist chapel at Beverley, of 1910.

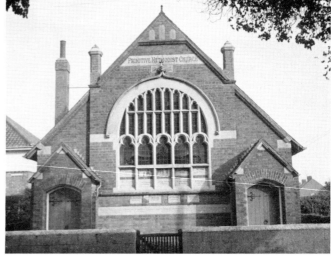

Welwick *Primitive Methodist chapel, 1911.*

TIN TABERNACLES

For rural congregations too poor during the Agricultural Depression to build in brick or stone or for urban congregations anxious to build a meeting place quickly to serve a new housing development the answer from the 1870s was a simple structure in timber and sheets of corrugated iron — the so-called 'tin tabernacle'.

The Wesleyan Chapel Committee at Manchester was not enthusiastic about the erection of iron chapels and in 1877 it was reluctant to support the building of a corrugated iron chapel at Arram, the first in the East Riding. Other 'tin tabernacles' were built at Bubwith (Quaker, 1879), Sutton on Derwent (Wesleyan, 1882), Kilnsea (Primitive, 1885), Goodmanham (Primitive, 1890), Enthorpe (Primitive, c.1912), and Yokefleet (Wesleyan, n.d.), and a wooden chapel was built at Aike (Primitive, 1885).

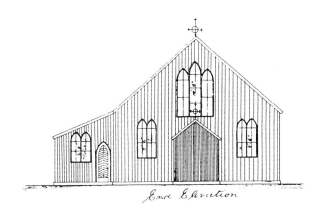

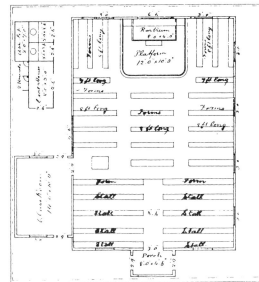

Plan and elevations for iron Wesleyan chapel at Beckside, Beverley 1880 (not built). (Humberside County Archives Office)

Goodmanham *Primitive chapel 1890. Still standing 1989.*

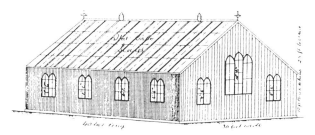

Millington Wesleyan Methodist chapel, 1900.
Foundation stone and initialled bricks.

Patrington Haven Primitive Methodist chapel.
Foundation stone laying 1905.

Welwick Primitive Methodist chapel, 1911.
Twenty-five foundation stones.

Coniston Primitive Methodist chapel.

STONE LAYING AND OPENING

For chapel builders the foundation stone laying and opening were the two key events when they hoped to raise funds to pay off part of the massive debt they had incurred. These events are fully reported in local newspapers and the official journals of the religious body concerned.

The Primitive Methodists in particular used the foundation stone laying as a major fund-raising event. At Lund £150 was raised on Good Friday 1871 when the foundation stone was laid for the new Primitive chapel. It became usual for more than one stone to be laid and later chapels abound in inscribed stones and lettered bricks. Those laying the stone or bricks each donated a sum of money. Thus £65 was raised in this way in June 1899 for Gilberdyke Primitive chapel when nine foundation stones and 34 bricks were laid. The identity of the principal stone layer was of major importance, for he or she would be expected to make the largest donation and also to be an attraction on the day. Members of the sect who had made high office or, as successful businessmen, were known benefactors were the obvious candidates.

In East Yorkshire and further afield members of the Hodge family from Hull laid more foundation stones for Primitive Methodist chapels than anybody else. They would donate at least £15 when they laid a stone. In 1861-3 William Hodge laid foundation stones at Peterborough and at East Dereham (Norfolk), his wife laid the stone at Cottingham, and their daughters laid stones at Broomfleet and at Kirton Lindsey (Lincs.). The family were particularly generous in Hull. When Henry Hodge laid the foundation stone of the Primitive chapel in Williamson Street in 1872 he handed over a £1,000 banknote. No wonder that at the first meeting to discuss the building of a Primitive Methodist chapel at Hotham in 1869 the trustees decided that 'Miss Hodge be requested to lay the stone'.

Withernsea. Opening of Wesleyan Methodist chapel, Queen Street, 1901.

Market Weighton Wesleyan Methodist chapel, 1868. Notice of opening services. (Humberside County Archives Office)

Chapel openings were similarly major occasions, with the associated events often lasting for a week or more. On the opening of Market Weighton Wesleyan chapel in 1868 seven services were held during the period 1 — 18 October. Amongst the preachers were the President and Secretary of the Conference and the most celebrated locally-born Wesleyan Thomas Jackson, then in his 85th year. This son of a Sancton agricultural labourer twice served as President of the Wesleyan Methodist Conference.

Newport. Interior of Wesleyan Methodist chapel. *(Drawing by Eugene Fisk).* One of the best surviving early Methodist chapel interiors in the East Riding. It retains the original three-sided gallery of 1814 with high-sided pews, rows of hat pegs, and Band of Hope banner. The pointed-arched windows, flanking the platform, as yet still look out on green fields.

Withernsea. Late 19th-century view of interior of Wesleyan chapel, Cammidge St., built in 1857. Closed 1900, demolished.

North Cave. Interior of Wesleyan chapel, Church St., built in 1839. Closed 1960.

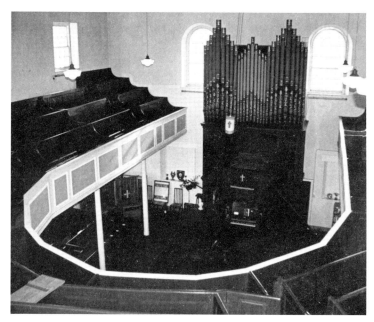

Cottingham Zion URC (Congregational) chapel. The little altered galleried interior of 1819.

CHAPEL INTERIORS

Nonconformist chapel interiors are largely simple rectangular auditoriums with a pulpit or preaching platform as the focal point. The woodwork and ironwork of the platform, galleries, communion rails and pews provide the main decorative features, along with the stove if it survives. Memorials and stained glass windows are rare.

In the larger chapels the visual dominance of the platform is usurped by the organ. Organs were allowed in Wesleyan chapels from 1820, but there was not wholehearted support for such 'popish instruments'. They were reluctantly accepted into Primitive chapels in the late 1850s. An organ was put up in Howden Wesleyan chapel in 1834 and that in Cottingham Zion chapel was installed in 1896.

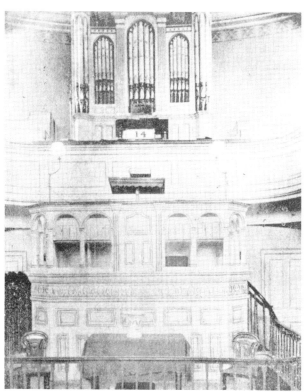

Howden. Interior of Wesleyan chapel as altered in 1846. Demolished 1974. (Postcard C. Ketchell)

Beverley Wesleyan chapel, Toll Gavel. Organ of 1890.

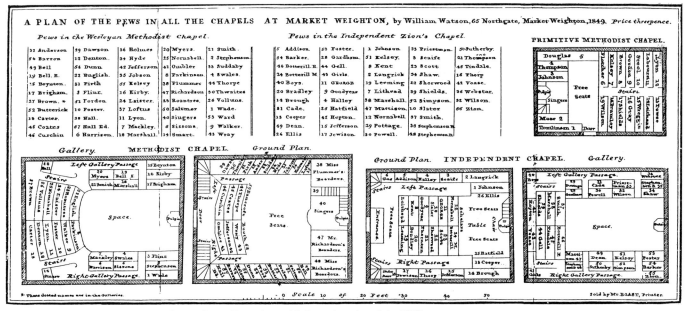

Market Weighton. Plans of pews in the Wesleyan, Primitive and Independent chapels by William Watson, surveyor, of Market Weighton, 1849. This plan provides a unique record of the interior arrangements and membership of all the nonconformist chapels in a small market town in the mid 19th century.

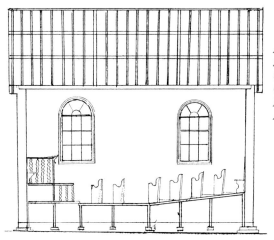

Allerthorpe Wesleyan chapel. Cross-section and ground plan, 1870. Unsigned but attributed to Thomas Grant, architect and builder, of Pocklington. (Humberside County Archives Office)

CHAPEL PLANS

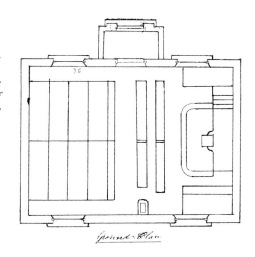

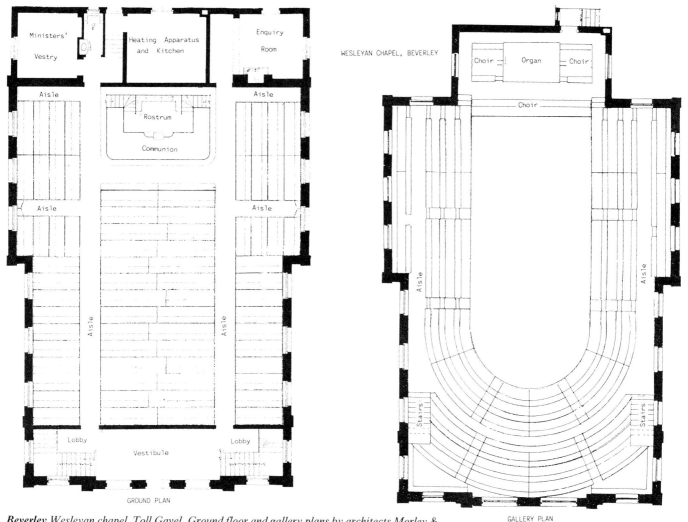

Beverley Wesleyan chapel, Toll Gavel. Ground floor and gallery plans by architects Morley & Woodhouse of Bradford, 1890. The chapel, which could seat over 900, cost £4,500 to build. (Humberside County Archives Office)

Over the 19th century the internal layout of chapels remained remarkably unchanged. The seating in the body of a chapel, and in the galleries fitted into larger buildings, was arranged so that the preacher could see, and be seen and heard by, his congregation. The pulpit or rostrum was usually at one end of the chapel, facing seating divided by two aisles. A central aisle, though not uncommon, was considered unsuitable as it was much better for the preacher to look directly upon his hearers than upon an open space.

Beverley Wesleyan Methodist chapel, Toll Gavel, 1890. Schoolrooms at rear 1903.

Bridlington Wesleyan Methodist Sunday school. Princess Street.

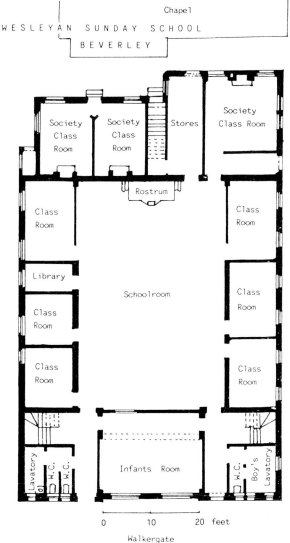

Beverley Wesleyan Methodist chapel, Toll Gavel. Plan of schoolrooms. Architect W. J. Morley, 1903. (Humberside County Archives Office)

SOCIAL AND EDUCATIONAL CENTRES

In 1850 the Revd. F. J. Jobson recommended that 'ministers and trustees, in their first meetings for the erection of a new chapel should consider that, as Methodists, they have not only to build a chapel, but also vestries, classrooms, and a larger room for prayer meetings, annual or other tea meetings, &c.'.

The nonconformist chapel was far from being just a place of worship on Sundays: it was also a social and educational centre for the whole week, with class meetings, band meetings, sewing meetings, prayer meetings, the Band of Hope, and above all the Sunday school. Sometimes the school was in a separate building but more often all the activities were accommodated under one roof. Many a large urban chapel has a rabbit warren of rooms to the rear of the building.

Withernwick Wesleyan Sunday school and inscription, 1845.

Great Driffield Primitive Methodist Sunday school, 1920.

Langtoft

From chapel to house – before and after.

South Dalton *Wesleyan chapel, 1825.*

Skelton, nr. Howden Wesleyan chapel, 1842. Unusual early castellated Gothic chapel before and after conversion to house.

CHAPEL CONVERSIONS

The majority of surviving chapel buildings listed in the following gazetteer are no longer used as places of worship. Some stand empty and derelict, threatened with demolition, but others have been converted to a modern use. Former chapels are now workshops, garages, shops, offices, warehouses, a cafe, and private houses. The regular plan of most chapels makes adaptation to a new use a simple procedure, yet in so many cases, particularly with conversion to a private house, too little account is taken of the architectural details which give character to the otherwise plain building. The original window and door openings, features that a good architect can capitalise on, are frequently destroyed.

A successful conversion. The former Harpham Wesleyan chapel of 1893. Photographed 1989.

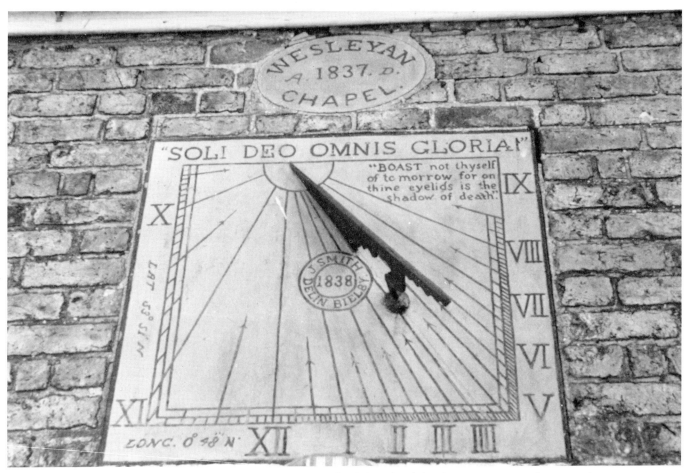

***Bielby** Wesleyan chapel, 1837. Sundial by J. Smith of Bielby, 1838. Chapel closed 1983 and converted to private house.*

APPENDIX A: GAZETTEER OF EAST RIDING CHAPELS AND MEETING HOUSES, 1689-1914

The gazetteer contains brief details of all East Riding nonconformist chapels and meeting houses known to have been built, or in use, between 1689 and 1914. Under each settlement all known chapel or meeting house sites are listed separately, followed by the original building date and the dates of subsequent rebuildings on that site. The final entry gives the date the chapel was recorded or last seen by members of the Nonconformist Building Recording Group

Abbreviations:

alt.	altered
arch.	architect
attrib.	attributed to
c.	circa
cl.	closed as chapel
dem.	demolished
der.	derelict
enl.	enlarged
ext.	extended
ho.	converted to house
lic.	licensed
n.d.	no date for building known
reb.	rebuilt on same site
rec.	date recorded or last seen by recorders
repl.	replaced
rest.	restored

ACKLAM (1) **Wesleyan** 1794, rest. 1909, arch. J. Butterworth, cl. 1966, now Anglican church, rec. 1985. (2) **Primitive** 1821, cl., stable, rec. 1985.

AIKE Primitive 1885, wooden, dem.

ALDBROUGH (1) **Wesleyan** 1828, reb. 1888, cl. 1961, store, rec. 1980. (2) **Primitive** 1850, enl. 1907, cl. 1960, store, rec. 1980.

ALLERTHORPE Wesleyan 1869, arch. T. Grant, cl. 1974, store, rec. 1988.

ANLABY (1) **Wesleyan** 1809, cl., store, rec. 1987.
(2) **Wesleyan** 1884, enl. 1956, in use, rec. 1987.
(3) **Primitive** n.d., dem.
(4) **Primitive** 1863, cl., office, rec. 1987.

ARRAM Wesleyan 1877, corrugated iron, cl. 1968, dem.

ASSELBY (1) **Wesleyan** 1810, cl., store, rec. 1989.
(2) **Wesleyan** 1868, cl. 1969, store, rec. 1988. (3) **Primitive** 1850, cl., ho., rec. 1989.

ATWICK (1) **Wesleyan** 1821, cl., ho., rec. 1987.
(2) **Primitive** 1856, cl. 1987, rec. 1987.

AUGHTON Wesleyan 1844, cl. by 1918, dem.

BAINTON (1) **Wesleyan** 1838, cl., rec. 1989, dem. 1990. (2) **Primitive** 1837, cl., store, rec. 1989.

BALKHOLME Primitive 1870, cl. c. 1950, ho., rec. 1979.

BARLBY Wesleyan 1857, dem. 1972.

BARMBY MARSH (1) **Wesleyan** 1813, rec. 1977, dem. later. (2) **Primitive** 1833, reb. 1902, arch. W. C. Smithson Leeds, in use, rec. 1989.

BARMBY MOOR (1) **Quaker** 1707, dem. (2) **Wesleyan** 1807, reb. 1869, arch. T. Grant, in use, rec. 1989. (3) **Primitive** 1834, cl. 1930s, ho., rec. 1989.

BARMSTON Wesleyan 1839, in use, rec. 1986.

BEEFORD (1) **Independent** 1810, enl. 1857, alt. 1880, cl., der., rec. 1988. (2) **Wesleyan**, before 1800, reb. 1866, in use, rec. 1988. (3) **Primitive** n.d., reb. 1873, arch. J. Wright, Hull, cl. 1964, rec. 1988.

BELLASIZE Wesleyan 1846, dem.

BEMPTON (1) **Wesleyan** 1825, reb. 1903, arch. S. Dyer, Bridlington, in use, rec. 1989. (2) **Primitive**, Ebenezer chap., 1843, enl. 1862, cl. 1964, store, rec. 1989.

BENTLEY Primitive 1895, cl. 1930s, dem. 1985.

BESWICK Primitive 1888, arch. attrib. W. Petch, Middleton, in use, rec. 1989.

BEVERLEY (1) **Presbyterian**, Lairgate by 1694, reb. 1704, destroyed in storm 1715, reb. 1715, congregation became **Independent** in later 18th cent., reb. 1800; reb. 1886 (Congregational), arch. T. B. Thompson, cl. 1976, dem. (2) **Congregational**, Shepherd Memorial mission chap., Grovehill, 1904, iron, enl., replaced 1935 by Latimer Memorial ch.

(3) **Quaker**, Lairgate, by 1702, reb. 1714. (4) **Quaker**, Wood Lane, c. 1810, cl. by 1840, dem.

(5) **Scotch Baptist**, Walkergate, 1808, cl. 1888, restaurant, rec. 1989. (6) **Scotch Baptist**, Wilbert Lane, 1888, arch. Hawe & Foley, cl. c. 1920, St. John Ambulance H.Q. from 1945, rec. 1989. (7) **Particular Baptist**, Well Lane, 1834, dem. 1909. (8) **Particular Baptist** Lord Roberts Rd., 1909-10, arch. G. F. Pennington, cl. c.1964, county library divisional H.Q., rec. 1989.

(9) **Methodist**, Wood Lane, 1781, cl. 1805. (10) **Wesleyan**, Walkergate, 1805, enl. 1836-7, repl. by Toll Gavel 1892, dem. 1903. (11) **Wesleyan**, Toll Gavel, 1890-1, arch. Morley & Woodhouse, Bradford, schoolroom 1903, arch. W. J. Morley & Sons, in use, (URC/Methodist), rec. 1989. (12) **Wesleyan**, Beckside, 1825, cl. 1882, dem. (13) **Wesleyan**, Flemingate, 1881-2, in use, rec. 1989. (14) **Wesleyan** (mission hall), Keldgate, 1899, cl. 1963, dem. c. 1971.
(15) **Primitive**, Wednesday Market, 1825, reb. 1867-8, arch. J. Wright, cl. 1955, dem. (16) **Primitive**, Norwood 1901, arch. J. C. Petch, Scarborough, in use, rec. 1989. (17) **Church Methodist**, Landress Lane, 1825, cl. c. 1830, dem. c. 1840, Congregational schoolroom built on site 1879. (18) **Wesleyan Reform**, (United Methodist Free Church from 1857), Trinity Lane, 1856, cl. 1926, Masonic Hall, rec. 1989. (19) **Salvation Army**, Wilbert Lane, 1885-6, arch. E. J. Sherwood, London, cl. 1985, dem. 1988.

Bewholme Primitive Methodist chapel, 1838.

BEWHOLME (1) **Wesleyan** 1835, cl., ho., rec. 1987. (2) **Primitive** 1838, enl. 1863, in use, rec. 1989.

BIELBY Wesleyan 1837, cl. 1983, ho., rec. 1986.

BISHOP BURTON (1) **Baptist** 1770, cl. c. 1955, dem. **Wesleyan** 1840, alt. 1896, rest. 1966, in use, rec. 1989.

BISHOP WILTON (1) **Wesleyan** 1810, alt. 1900-1, arch. G. F. Danby, cl. 1974, rec. 1985. (2) **Primitive** 1835, enl. 1863, cl. by 1941, shop, rec. 1985.

BLACKTOFT Wesleyan 1839, arch. J. Shaw, in use 1979, cl., der., rec. 1988.

BOLTON (1) **Wesleyan** 1819, cl. 1869, dem. (2) **Wesleyan** 1869, arch. T. Grant, in use, rec. 1989. Burial ground.

BRANDESBURTON (1) **Independent** 1809, bought by **Primitives** 1856, enl. 1863, cl., ho., rec. 1988. (2) **Wesleyan** 1809, cl., ho., rec. 1988. (3) **Primitive**, Moor Town, 1870, cl., rec. 1988.

BREIGHTON Wesleyan 1864, dem.

BRIDLINGTON (1) **Presbyterian**, meeting began 1662, first purpose built meeting house 1698, dem.
(2) **Presbyterian (Independent)**, Zion chap., St. John St., soon after 1700, enl. c. 1790, rest. 1886, cl. 1906, dem. Burial ground. (3) **Congregational**, Zion chap., St. John St., 1906, arch. J. Shepherdson, in use, rec. 1989.
(4) **Congregational**, Union chap., Prospect St., 1817, cl. 1840, dem. (5) **Congregational**, Trinity ch., Promenade, 1879, arch. J. Earnshaw, cl. 1970s, der., r. 1989.

Bubwith Wesleyan chapel, 1796. Demolished c. 1975.

(6) **Quaker**, St. John St., 1678, cl. 1784, reopened 1810, deregistered 1861, dem. (7) **Quaker**, Havelock St., 1903, iron and wood, dem. 1983.

(8) **Baptist**, Applegarth Lane, 1699, cl. c. 1713, rec. 1989. Burial ground. (9) **Baptist**, Bayle Gate, c. 1713, cl. 1874, dem. Burial ground. (10) **Baptist**, Quay Road, 1874, arch. S. Musgrave, Hull, front part dem., rec. 1989.

(11) **Wesleyan**, St. John St., 1775, reb. 1803, enl. 1805, cl. 1884, shop, rec. 1989. (12) **Wesleyan**, Burlington chap., St. John St., 1884, arch. J. Earnshaw, in use, rec. 1989. (13) **Wesleyan**, Chapel St., 1795, enl. 1818 and 1820, reb. 1873, arch. W. Botterill, Hull, in use, rec. 1989. (14) **Primitive**, St. John St., 1833, cl. 1849, dem. (15) **Primitive**, St. John St., 1849, reb. 1877 (St. John's Meth. ch.), arch. W. Freeman, Hull, cl. 1970, shop, rec. 1989. (16) **Primitive**. Esplanade, 1833, cl., dem. 1869. (17) **Primitive**, Chapel St., 1870, arch., J. Wright, Hull, reb. 1879 (Central Meth. ch.), arch. W. Freeman, Hull, cl. 1969, dem. (18) **Wesleyan Reform**, Promenade, 1852, arch. G. Truelove, reb. 1872, arch. J. Earnshaw became **United Methodist Free Church**, deregistered 1958, dem. (19) **Salvation Army**, Wellington Rd., 1887, former Temperance Hall, (built 1876-7 arch. J. Earnshaw), in use, rec. 1989.

BRIGHAM Wesleyan 1819, cl. 1950s, ho., rec. 1988.

BROOMFLEET (1) **Wesleyan** 1822, cl. 1965, dem.
(2) **Primitive** 1861, cl. 1930s, store, rec. 1988.

BROUGH Wesleyan 1852, cl., cafe/ho., rec. 1986.

BUBWITH (1) **Quaker** 1879, corrugated iron, removed to Sunk Island. (2) **Wesleyan** 1796, enl. 1870, dem. c. 1975. (3) **Primitive** n.d., repl. 1862, arch. T. Pratt, cl., hall, rec. 1977.

BUGTHORPE (1) **Wesleyan** 1840, former schoolroom,

cl., rec. 1980. (2) **Primitive** 1833, former schoolroom, cl., dem.

BURSTWICK (1) **Wesleyan** 1847, cl. c. 1920, ho., rec. 1980. (2) **Primitive** 1826, reb. 1848, cl. 1898, ho., rec. 1980. (3) **Primitive** 1898, arch. T. B. Thompson, in use, rec. 1980.

BURTON AGNES **Wesleyan** 1837, cl. 1985, ho., rec. 1988.

BURTON FLEMING (1) **Wesleyan** 1806, reb. 1883, in use, rec. 1987. (2) **Primitive** 1838, cl., store, rec. 1987. (3) **Primitive** 1903, cl., ho., rec. 1987.

BURTON PIDSEA **Wesleyan** 1820, reb. 1847, rest. 1909, cl. 1970, n.k., rec. 1980.

BURYTHORPE (1) **Wesleyan** 1820, rest. 1902, cl., garage, rec. 1984. (2) **United Free Methodist Church** 1865, dem.

CARNABY **Wesleyan** 1876, cl., 1964, ho., rec. 1986.

CATTON (High) (1) **Wesleyan** 1805/10, cl. 1901, ho., rec. 1989. (2) **Wesleyan** 1900, arch. G. F. Danby, Leeds, cl. 1974, rec. 1989. (3) **Primitive** 1856, cl. c. 1930, ho., rec. 1989.

CATWICK (1) **Wesleyan** 1838, cl., n.k., rec. 1988. (2) **Primitive** 1839, dem.

CHERRY BURTON (1) **Church Methodist/Wesleyan** 1825, cl. 1920s, village hall 1928, rec. 1986. (2) **Primitive** 1844/51, cl. 1964, dem.

CLIFFE cum LUND (1) **Wesleyan** 1825, cl. 1969, dem. (2) **Primitive** 1842, reb. 1864, cl., store, rec. 1989.

CONISTON **Primitive** 1872, arch. F. N. Pettingell, in use, rec. 1989.

COTTINGHAM (1) **Presbyterian** (later Independent then Congregational), Hallgate, by 1697, reb. 1819, arch. Appleton Bennison, in use, (URC), rec. 1989.
(2) **Wesleyan**, Northgate 1783, former barn, reb. 1803, enl. 1814, cl. 1879, dem. 1950s. (3) **Wesleyan**, Hallgate, 1878-9, arch. W. Ranger, in use, rec. 1989. (4) **Primitive**, Hallgate, 1825, cl. 1861, dem. (5) **Primitive**, King St., 1861, arch. J. Wright, alt. 1915, cl. 1937, office, rec. 1989. (6) **Salvation Army**, Northgate, 1888, cl. 1959, dem.

DEIGHTON (1) **Wesleyan** 1880, in use, rec. 1989.

DUGGLEBY (1) **Wesleyan** 1826, reb. 1856, arch. F. Jobson, cl., ho., rec. 1988. (2) **Primitive** 1835, rest. 1865, cl., dem.

DUNNINGTON (Holderness) (1) **Wesleyan** 1858, cl. c. 1970, store, rec. 1987. (2) **Primitive** 1839, cl., dem.

DUNNINGTON (York) (1) **Wesleyan**, York St., 1805, cl. 1868, dem. (2) **Wesleyan**, Common Lane, 1868, in use, rec. 1988. (3) **Primitive** 1852, cl., ho., rec. 1988.

DUNSWELL **Methodist New Connexion** 1817, cl. 1968, store, rec. 1987.

EASINGTON (1) **Wesleyan** 1850, rest. 1901, in use, rec. 1980. (2) **Primitive** 1822, cl. 1851, dem. (3) **Primitive** 1851, alt. 1855, cl. 1964, rec. 1980.

EAST COTTINGWITH (1) **Quaker** 1788, cl., rec. 1989. Burial ground. (2) **Wesleyan** 1796, enl. 1868, cl. 1973, store, rec. 1989.

EAST HESLERTON **Wesleyan** 1794, enl. 1840, in use, rec. 1987.

EASTRINGTON (1) **Wesleyan** 1827, rest. 1871, reb. 1893, arch. A. Gelder, in use, rec. 1989. (2) **Primitive** 1871, cl. 1923, part. dem., ho., rec. 1979.

Fangfoss Wesleyan chapel, 1865.

ELLERBY (Old) Wesleyan 1838, cl., dem.

ELLERBY (New) Wesleyan 1909, in use, rec. 1989.

ELLERKER Wesleyan Reform 1850, became **Primitive** 1856, cl., disused shop, rec. 1988.

ELLERTON (1) **Wesleyan** 1811, in use, rec. 1988. (2) **Primitive** 1863-4, cl., dem.

ELLOUGHTON (1) **Independent (Congregational)** 1814, reb. 1876-7, arch. S. Musgrave, in use (URC), rec. 1988. (2) **Quaker**, location and date of possible late 17th cent. meeting house unknown. Burial ground. (3) **Primitive** 1830, reb. 1866, cl. 1958, store, rec. 1988.

ELSTRONWICK Primitive 1853, in use, rec. 1980.

ELVINGTON Wesleyan 1810, rest. 1833 and 1899, arch. G. F. Danby, cl. after 1972, store, rec. 1984.

ENTHORPE Primitive c.1912, corrugated iron, cl., moved to Arras 1972.

ETTON Primitive 1845, rest. 1884, cl. 1968, rebuilt as garage by 1976.

FANGFOSS (1) **Wesleyan** 1837, reb. 1865, cl. 1974, workshop, rec. 1989. (2) **Primitive** 1865, cl. by 1947, workshop, rec. 1989.

FAXFLEET (1) **Wesleyan** 1843, reb. 1849, cl. 1912, cottages, rec. 1984. (2) **Primitive**, at brickworks, 1850, cl., dem.

FILEY (1) **Wesleyan**, off Queen St., 1811, dem. (2) **Wesleyan**, Murray St., 1838-9, enl. 1859, cl. 1876, dem. (3) **Wesleyan**, Trinity chap., Union St., 1876, burnt

1918, rest. 1923, in use, rec. 1988. (4) **Primitive** Bethesda chap., Mitford st., 1823, enl. 1843 and 1859, cl. 1870, became Albert Hall, dem. after 1970. (5) **Primitive** Ebenezer chap., Union St., 1870-1, arch. J. Wright, cl., shop/store, rec. 1988.

FIMBER (1) **Wesleyan** n.d., reb. 1863, cl., dem. 1948. (2) **Primitive** 1839, reb. 1863, cl., dem. 1975.

FLAMBOROUGH (1) **Wesleyan** 1799, cl. 1889,. became Liberal Hall, dem. (2) **Wesleyan** 1889, arch. J. Earnshaw, cl. 1965, rec. 1988, dem. 1989. (3) **Primitive** 1821, repl. 1874, arch. J. Wright, cl. 1968, dem.

FLINTON Wesleyan 1855, disused c.1973, rec. 1978, reb. as garage 1979-80.

FLIXTON (1) **Wesleyan** 1841, cl. c. 1939, ho., rec. 1988. (2) **Primitive** 1821, cl. 1841, cottage in 1971. (3) **Primitive** 1841, cl. after 1971, rec. 1988.

FOGGATHORPE Wesleyan 1803, also used as day school, cl. 1922, dem.

FOSTON (1) **Independent** Bethel chap., 1814, cl. 1865, shell remained 1989. (2) **Wesleyan** 1802, cl. 1879, became village hall 1923-4, dem. (3) **Wesleyan** 1879, arch. J. Earnshaw, cl. 1967, store, rec. 1989.

FOXHOLES Wesleyan 1820, reb. 1872, cl., rec. 1985.

FRIDAYTHORPE (1) **Wesleyan** 1840, cl., der., rec. 1987. (2) **Primitive** 1851, cl. 1932, ho., rec. 1987.

FULFORD (1) **Wesleyan**, School Lane, 1820, cl. 1845, store, rec. 1987. (2) **Wesleyan**, Main St., 1845, reb. 1896, in use, rec. 1987.

FULL SUTTON Wesleyan 1828-9, cl. 1974, ho., rec. 1989.

GANTON Wesleyan by 1877 in cottage, ext., cl. 1970, ho., rec. 1989.

GARTON (Holderness) Wesleyan 1826, cl. 1934, dem.

GARTON ON THE WOLDS (1) **Wesleyan** 1786, reb. 1809, 1854, and 1894, cl. by 1988, ho., rec. 1989. (2) **Primitive** 1824, reb. 1871, arch J. Wright, cl. by 1954, workshop, rec. 1989.

GEMBLING Primitive 1845, cl. by 1954, dem.

GILBERDIKE (1) **Wesleyan** 1846, dem. (2) **Wesleyan** 1895, in use, rec. 1987. (3) **Primitive** 1846, cl. 1899, ho., rec. 1979. (4) **Primitive** 1899, cl., workshop, rec. 1987.

GOODMANHAM (1) **Wesleyan** 1828, cl. 1961, ho., rec. 1989. (2) **Primitive** 1890, corrugated iron, cl. store, rec. 1989.

GRANSMOOR Wesleyan 1839, reb. 1924.

GREAT COWDEN Wesleyan 1835, dem.

GREAT DRIFFIELD (1) **Independent (Congregational)**, Exchange St., 1802, reb. 1866-7, arch. H. J. Paull, in use, rec. 1989. (2) **Baptist**, King St., 1788, cl. 1861, hall, rec. 1988. (3) **Baptist**, Middle St. South, 1861, arch. W. Hawe, new front 1884, arch. J. F. Shepherdson, dem.
(4) **Wesleyan**, Westgate, 1777, cl. 1828, became Mechanics' Institute, dem. (5) **Wesleyan**, Middle St. North, 1828, alt. 1862, arch. W. Hawe, repl. 1880, arch. H. J. Paull, in use, rec. 1989. (6) **Primitive**, Mill St., 1821, enl. 1856, alt. 1865, arch. H. Fippard, cl. 1873, dem. 1980s. (7) **Primitive**, George St., 1873, arch. J. Wright, cl. 1964, front dem., warehouse, rec. 1989. (9) **Wesleyan Reform (United Methodist Free Church)**, Bridge St., 1863, arch. C. E. Taylor, cl., showroom, rec. 1989.

GREAT HATFIELD (1) **Wesleyan** 1838, cl., dem.

(2) **Primitive** 1862, enl. 1901, in use, rec. 1987.

GREAT KELK (1) **Wesleyan** 1814, cl. 1894, rec. 1989.
(2) **Wesleyan** 1894, in use, rec. 1989.

GRINDALE (1) **Wesleyan** 1826, reb. 1861, arch. R. G. Smith, Hull, cl. by 1954, village hall 1969, store, rec. 1989.
(2) **Primitive** c.1845, dem.

HAISTHORPE Primitive 1888, in use, rec. 1989.

Halsham

HALSHAM Primitive 1873, arch. W. Freeman, in use, rec. 1980.

HARLTHORPE Wesleyan, n.d., cl., part dem., rec. 1977.

HARPHAM Wesleyan 1893, cl. 1985, ho., rec. 1989.

HAYTON Primitive 1830, reb. 1850, cl. 1919, dem. 1968.

HEDON (1) **Baptist**, Magdalen Gate, 1801, used by Wesleyans 1812-18 and Primitives 1819-73, cl. c. 1910, British Legion Club, rec. 1989. (2) **Wesleyan**, George St., 1818, reb. 1875, arch. J. T. Webster, Hedon, cl. 1948, dem. (3) **Primitive**, Baxter Gate, 1873, arch. F. N. Pettingell, enl. 1883 (schoolroom), destroyed by bomb 1917.

HELPERTHORPE Wesleyan 1852, rest. 1899, cl. 1968, store, rec. 1984.

HEMINGBROUGH (1) **Wesleyan** 1836, reb. 1848, in use, rec. 1989. (2) **Primitive** 1857, store, rec. 1989.

HESLINGTON (1) **New Wesleyan Methodist Association** 1832, in use 1851, dem. (2) **Wesleyan** 1844, cl. 1949, hall, rec. 1989. (3) **Independent Methodist**, 1847, acquired by **Primitive Methodists** by 1887, dem. since 1972.

HESSLE (1) **Congregational**, Trinity chapel, Station Lane, 1900, largely reb., in use (URC), rec. 1989.
(2) **Wesleyan**, Dead Man's Lane, n.d., dem. (3) **Wesleyan**, Vicarage Lane, 1813, cl. 1877, ho., rec. 1988. (4) **Wesleyan**, Tower Hill, 1876-7 arch. W. Botterill, in use, rec. 1988.
(5) **Primitive**, Chapel Yard, Southgate, 1827, reb. 1857,

Hessle Primitive Methodist chapel, South Lane, 1909.

arch. J. Wright, cl. 1909, dem. (6) **Primitive**, South Lane, 1909, arch. T. B. Atkinson, cl. by 1978 showroom, rec. 1988. (7) **United Methodist Free Church**, Northgate, 1863, cl., dem. 1970s. (8) **Wesleyan**, Hessle Cliff, c. 1865, dem. (9) **Wesleyan**, Springville, 1879, enl. 1904, in use, rec. 1989.

HOLLYM (1) **Wesleyan** 1805, reb. 1824, cl. c. 1875, dem. (2) **Primitive** 1860, cl. 1979, store, rec. 1980.

HOLME UPON SPALDING MOOR (1) **Wesleyan** 1787, reb. 1827, in use, rec. 1989. (2) **Primitive** 1850, reb. 1880, cl. 1986, rec. 1986.

HOLMPTON (1) **Wesleyan** 1820, reb. 1878, sold to **Primitives** 1906, cl. 1932, ho., rec. 1980. (2) **Primitive** n.d., cl. 1905, workshop, rec. 1989.

HORNSEA (1) **Independent (Congregational)**, Southgate, 1808, cl. 1873, became Church Mission Hall, der., rec. 1989. (2) **Congregational**, New Road, 1872-3, arch. S. Musgrave, in use (URC), rec. 1989. (3) **Quaker**, meeting house registered 1711, possibly the cottage in Back Westgate owned by Soc. of Friends from 1750 and still available for worship, rec. 1989. (4) **Wesleyan**, Back Southgate, 1814, cl. 1870, store, rec. 1989. (5) **Wesleyan**, Newbegin, 1870, arch. J. K. James, Hull, in use, rec. 1989. (6) **Primitive**, Market Place, 1835, reb. 1864-5, arch. J. Wright, cl., flats, r. 1990.

HOTHAM Primitive 1869, arch. J. Wright, in use 1986, cl., sold 1989.

HOWDEN (1) **Independent (Congregational)**, Bridgegate, 1722, reb. 1795, enl. 1837, arch. Sharpe, York, refronted 1878, arch. Shaw Bros., Howden, dem. c. 1979. (2) **Wesleyan**, Hailgate, 1786, reb. 1832, enl. 1835 and 1846, dem. 1974. (3) **Primitive**, St. John St., 1837, cl. 1872, schoolroom, dem. 1988. (4) **Primitive**, St. John St., 1872, cl., dem. 1988. (5) **Inghamite**, Hailgate, 1820, dem. 1985.

HUGGATE (1)**Wesleyan** 1837, cl. 1885, hos., rec. 1987. (2) **Wesleyan** 1885, cl. 1974, ho., rec. 1987. (3) **Primitive** 1849, cl., dem. 1980s.

HUMBLETON Primitive 1860, in use, rec. 1980.

HUNMANBY (1) **Baptist**. Hungate Lane, 1816, cl. by 1870s, dem. since 1970. (2) **Wesleyan**, Stonegate, lic. 1816, cl. 1871, ho., rec. 1988. (3) **Wesleyan**, Bridlington St., 1871, cl. 1958, shop, rec. 1988. (4) **Primitive**, Hungate Lane, 1841, cl. 1964, dem.

HUTTON CRANSWICK (1) **Quaker**, 1706-7, dem. (2) **Baptist** 1841, reb. 1880, cl., hall, rec. 1989. (3) **Wesleyan** c. 1800, cl. 1861, became Oddfellows Hall 1862, now ho., rec. 1989. (4) **Wesleyan** Trinity chap. 1861, arch. W. Hawe, in use, rec. 1989. (5) **Primitive** 1836, reb. 1864, cl. 1969, dem. 1970. (6) **Primitive** (Hutton) 1860, in use, rec. 1989.

KELFIELD (1) **Wesleyan** 1815, in use, rec. 1989. (2) **Primitive** 1852, cl. by 1894, der., rec. 1989.

KEYINGHAM (1) **Wesleyan** 1807, cl. 1848. (2) **Wesleyan** 1848, Chapel Lane, cl. 1932, dem. (3) **Primitive** 1823, Main St., cl. 1846, ho., rec. 1980. (4) **Primitive** 1846, Ings Lane, reb. 1909, arch. T. B. Atkinson, reb. 1973, arch. B. Blanchard, in use, rec. 1980.

KILHAM (1) **Baptist**, Baptist St., 1819, cl. c. 1920, dem. (2) **Wesleyan** Middle St., 1789, repl. 1815, reb. 1907, in use, rec. 1988. (3) **Primitive**, Middle St., 1824, cl. 1860. (4) **Primitive**, Baptist St., 1860, cl. 1946, dem.

KILNSEA Primitive 1885, corrugated iron. cl. by 1920, ho. (Hodge Villa), rec. 1979.

KILNWICK Primitive, former National School built 1821, used as chapel after 1874, cl. 1963, ho., rec. 1989.

KILPIN Wesleyan 1867, arch. W. Johnson, Howden, cl.

Kelfield Wesleyan chapel, 1815.

1912, ho., rec. 1987.

KIRBY GRINDALYTHE Wesleyan 1886, disused, rec. 1984.

KIRKBURN Primitive 1839, reb. 1899, cl. by 1974, workshop, rec. 1989.

KNAPTON Quaker and Wesleyan, by 1815, former barn, in use by Methodists, rec. 1989.

LANGTOFT (1) **Wesleyan** 1808, cl. 1875, Sunday school, rec. 1988. (2) **Wesleyan** 1874, arch. W. Ranger, in use, rec. 1988. (3) **Primitive** 1839, cl. c. 1950, ho., rec. 1988.

LANGTON Wesleyan 1821, rest. 1839, cl., dem.

LAXTON Wesleyan 1848, cl. by 1941, garage, rec. 1979.

LEAVENING (1) **Wesleyan** 1824, in use, rec. 1984. (2) **Primitive** 1821, rest. c. 1880, cl., dem.

LELLEY Wesleyan 1859, cl. 1968, dem.

LEPPINGTON Wesleyan 1835, reb. 1867, arch. T. Grant, in use, rec. 1985.

LEVEN (1) **Independent** 1809, dem. (2) **Wesleyan** 1816, enl. 1835, rest. 1889, dem. (3) **Primitive** 1836, repl. 1877, dem.

LITTLE DRIFFIELD Primitive 1878, arch. W. Petch, der., rec. 1989.

LITTLE KELK Primitive 1861, cl. 1962, ho., rec. 1989.

LITTLE WEIGHTON Wesleyan 1827, in use, rec. 1987.

LOCKINGTON (1) **Wesleyan** 1812, reb. 1879, arch. J. F. Shepherdson, in use, rec. 1989. (2) **Primitive** 1825, reb. 1862, arch. W. Petch, enl. 1913, disused, rec. 1989.

LONG RISTON (1) **Independent** 1837 replacing former barn lic. 1803, taken over by Wesleyans, cl., store, rec. 1986. (2) **Primitive** 1836, cl. in 1977, der., rec. 1986.

LUND (1) **Wesleyan** 1835, cl., part dem., ho., rec. 1986. (2) **Primitive** 1839, cl. 1871, later Oddfellows Hall, now Church Hall, rec. 1989. (3) **Primitive** 1871, arch. attrib. W. Petch, Middleton, in use, rec. 1986.

LUTTONS AMBO (1) **Wesleyan** 1817, rest. 1880, in use, rec. 1987. (2) **Primitive** 1848, reb. 1863, cl., dem.

MAPPLETON Independent and Wesleyan 1828, repl. 1890, cl. 1967, village hall, rec. 1987.

MARFLEET Wesleyan 1872, cl. by 1906, workshop, rec. 1985.

MARKET WEIGHTON (1) **Independent (Congregational)** 1809, reb. 1881, arch. J. Sulman, London, cl., shop, rec. 1989. (2) **Wesleyan** 1786, cl. 1868, worksahop, rec. 1989. (3) **Wesleyan** 1868, arch. W. Botterill, Hull, in use, rec.

53

1989. (4) **Primitive** 1828, reb. 1860, cl., office, rec. 1989. (5) **Primitive** 1902, arch. W. Smithson, Leeds, cl., shop, rec. 1989.

MEAUX Independent, Bethel chap., 1823, became **Methodist New Connexion** by 1851, cl., dem.

MELBOURNE (1) **Wesleyan** 1811, in use, rec. 1988. (2) **Primitive** 1821, enl. 1859, cl. 1930s, hall, rec. 1977.

MIDDLETON (1) **Wesleyan** 1809, cl. 1902, ho., rec. 1987. (2) **Wesleyan** 1902, in use, rec. 1987. (3) **Wesleyan**, Wold Cottages, 1847, cl., ho., rec. 1987. (4) **Primitive** 1821, cl. 1864, dem. (5) **Primitive** 1864-5, arch. H. Fippard, York, cl., ho., rec. 1987.

MILLINGTON (1) **Wesleyan** 1803, repl. 1900, arch. G. F. Danby, in use, rec. 1987. (2) **Primitive** 1866, cl. 1939, ho., rec. 1987.

MUSTON (1) **Independent (Congregational)**, Providence chap., 1815, cl. c. 1972, store, rec. 1988. (2) **Wesleyan** 1866, wooden, dem. by 1970. (3) **Primitive** 1824, in use, rec. 1988.

NABURN (1) **Wesleyan** 1818, cl. 1857, ho., rec. 1989. (2) **Wesleyan** 1857, cl. 1970, dem.

NAFFERTON (1) **Baptist and Independent**, Union chap., Westgate, 1821, taken over by Wesley Reformers, cl. 1860s, dem. (2) **Wesleyan**, 1792, reb. 1839 and 1907, in use, rec. 1989. (3) **Primitive**, Priestgate, 1824, cl. 1858, dem. (4) **Primitive**, Coppergate, 1858, arch. J. Wright, cl. 1967, dem. 1988.

NEWLAND (Cottingham, now Hull) (1) **Wesleyan**, Newland Ave., 1857-58, arch. W. Botterill, enl. 1867 and 1889, arch. W. Botterill, cl. 1901. (2) **Wesleyan**, Newland Ave., 1901, arch. Gelder & Kitchen, repl. 1928.

NEWPORT (1) **Wesleyan** 1789, cl. 1814, became Sunday school, rec. 1989. (2) **Wesleyan** 1814, in use, rec. 1989. (3) **Primitive** 1827, cl. 1891, parish room, dem. (4) **Primitive** Walmsley Memorial chap., 1891, cl., dem. 1984, rec. 1979.

NEWTON ON DERWENT Wesleyan 1818, reb. 1901, arch. G. F. Danby, in use, rec. 1989.

NORTH CAVE (1) **Quaker** 1687, cottage used as meeting house, reb. 1793, cl. 1865, dem. c. 1888. Burial ground (14 Church St.). (2) **Wesleyan**, Westgate, 1823, cl., school, dem. (3) **Wesleyan**, Church St., 1839, cl. 1960, store, rec. 1988. (4) **Primitive**, Church St., 1819, cl. 1870, dem. (5) **Primitive**, Westgate, 1870, arch. J. Wright, in use, rec. 1989.

NORTH DALTON (1) **Wesleyan** 1839, ext. 1870, cl. 1975, ho., rec. 1987. (2) **Primitive** 1836, reb. 1867, dem. c. 1965.

NORTH DUFFIELD (1) **Wesleyan** 1833, cl. 1876, Sunday school, rec. 1987. (2) **Wesleyan** 1876, in use, rec. 1987. (3) **Primitive** 1821, cl. 1926-7, ho., rec. 1977.

NORTH FERRIBY (1) **Primitive** 1828, cl. 1877, Oddfellows Hall until 1987, now ho., rec. 1989. (2) **Primitive** 1877, in use, rec. 1989.

NORTH FRODINGHAM (1) **Independent (Congregational)**, 1820, alt. 1858, rest. 1878, arch. J. F. Shepherdson, cl., dem., rec. 1983. (2) **Wesleyan**, by 1800, cl., Sunday school, rec. 1983. (3) **Wesleyan** 1891, in use, rec. 1983. (4) **Primitive** 1842, cl., part dem., workshop, rec. 1983.

NORTH NEWBALD (1) **Baptist**, Eastgate, 1867, cl. 1955, ho., rec. 1987. (2) **Baptist**, Galegate, 1874, cl. by 1894, parish hall, dem. (3) **Wesleyan**, Burgate, 1805, cl. 1932, garage/store, rec. 1987. (4) **Primitive**, Galegate, 1839, cl. 1878, ho., rec. 1987. (5) **Primitive**, Ratten row,

Patrington Wesleyan chapel, 1811. Refronted late 19th century.

1878, cl. 1956, dem. 1987.

NORTON (1) **Wesleyan** 1839, repl. 1857, arch. W. Lovel, Norton, in use, rec. 1985. (2) **Primitive** 1864, arch. J. Gibson, Malton, ext. 1884, in use, rec. 1985. (3) **Salvation Army**, Wood St., n.d., rec. 1985.

NUNBURNHOLME Wesleyan 1828, reb. 1879, arch. W. Ranger, London, cl. 1974, dem., rec. 1979.

OTTRINGHAM (1) **Wesleyan** 1815, cl. 1856, Sunday school, rec. 1980. (2) **Wesleyan** 1856, rest. 1902, in use, rec. 1980.

OWSTWICK (1) **Quaker** c. 1670, cl. c. 1840, dem. after 1911. (2) **Wesleyan**, by 1892, former cottage, cl. 1979, rec. 1980.

PATRINGTON (1) **Independent** 1802, cl. by 1840, dem. (2) **Wesleyan** Greenshaw Lane, 1811, reb. late 19th cent., in use, rec. 1988. (3) **Primitive**, Greenshaw Lane, 1841, reb. 1862, arch. J. Wright, cl. 1932, store, rec. 1988. (4) **Primitive**, Patrington Haven 1852, cl. 1905, store, rec. 1980. (5) **Primitive**, Patrington Haven, 1905, arch. T. B. Atkinson, in use, rec. 1980.

PAULL (1) **Wesleyan** 1805, rest. 1912, in use, rec. 1980. (2) **Primitive** 1851, cl. 1871, dem. (3) **Primitive** 1871, cl. 1915, ho., rec. 1980.

POCKLINGTON (1) **Independent (Congregational)**, Chapmangate, 1807, reb. 1879, arch. T. B. Thompson, in use (Pentecostal), rec. 1989. (2) **Wesleyan**, Chapmangate, former barn, 1762, reb. 1795, 1813, and 1864, arch. E. Taylor, in use, rec. 1989. (3) **Primitive**, Chapmangate, 1820, arch. H. Ibbotson, Pocklington, cl. 1865, dem. (4) **Primitive**, Union St., 1865, cl. 1964, dem. 1979.

PORTINGTON Wesleyan before 1800, reb. 1866, cl. 1912, der., rec. 1987.

PRESTON (1) **Baptist**, School Rd., 1828, cl. 1850, dem. (2) **Wesleyan**, Main St., 1812, repl. 1898, ho. and schoolroom, rec. 1978. (3) **Wesleyan**, Station Rd., 1898, in use, rec. 1980. (4) **Primitive**, School Rd., 1822, enl. 1858, reb. 1867, arch. attrib. J. Wright, cl. c. 1955, hall and workshop, rec. 1980. (5) **Primitive**, Hull Rd., by 1911, cl. by 1934, dem.

REIGHTON Wesleyan 1818, enl. 1857, cl. 1925, dem.

RICCALL (1) **Wesleyan**, Chapel Lane, 1798, cl., 1864, dem. 1972. (2) **Wesleyan**, Main St., 1864, in use, rec. 1989. (3) **Primitive**, Main St., n.d., repl. 1857, arch. Mr. Pratt, cl. 1930s, store, rec. 1989.

Rillington Bethesda chapel, 1818.

RILLINGTON (1) **Independent (Congregational)** 1818, rest. 1875, cl., der., rec. 1989. (2) **Wesleyan** 1805, in use, rec. 1984. (3) **Primitive** 1832, reb. 1880, cl., in use, rec. 1984.

RIMSWELL (1) **Primitive** c. 1813, reb. 1889, dem. (2) **Primitive** 1889, cl. 1965, ho., rec. 1980.

ROOS (1) **Wesleyan** 1808, rest. c. 1854, cl. c. 1968, dem. 1977. (2) **Primitive** 1826, repl. 1868, arch. J. Wright, cl., dem. c. 1970.

ROTSEA Wesleyan 1847, dem.

RUDSTON (1) **Wesleyan** 1811, reb. 1879, arch. J. Earnshaw, cl. by 1939, village hall, rec. 1989. (2) **Primitive** 1830, reb. 1877, arch. Rev. A. J. Noble, in use, rec. 1989.

RUSTON PARVA Wesleyan 1810, cl. 1962, dem.

RYHILL Wesleyan 1819, reb. 1897, cl. 1965, ho., rec. 1980.

SANCTON Wesleyan 1815, enl. 1840, in use, rec. 1986.

SANDHOLME (Gilberdike) Wesleyan c. 1810, cl., store, rec. 1987.

SCAGGLETHORPE (1) **Wesleyan** c. 1816, cl., ho., rec. 1984. (2) **Primitive** 1866, cl., dem.

SEATON (1) **Wesleyan** 1810, enl. 1878, cl., dem. (2) **Primitive** 1837, in use, rec. 1988.

SEATON ROSS (1) **Wesleyan** 1822, reb. 1900, arch. G. F. Danby, cl., ho., rec. 1989. (2) **Primitive** 1821, reb. 1878, cl. 1965, store, rec. 1989.

SETTRINGTON Wesleyan 1890, arch. C. H. Channon, Malton, in use, rec. 1989.

SEWERBY Wesleyan 1825, cl. and dem. 1962.

SHERBURN (1) **Wesleyan** 1813, enl. 1865, Sunday school 1882, in use, rec. 1984. (2) **Primitive** 1865, cl., dem.

SHIPTONTHORPE (1) **Wesleyan** 1833, dem. 1967. (2) **Primitive** 1834, reb. 1867, cl., ho., rec. 1986.

SKEFFLING (1) Wesleyan 1822, cl. 1870, dem.
(2) Wesleyan 1870, cl. c. 1960, farm building, rec. 1980.

SKELTON Wesleyan 1842, cl. 1960, ho., rec. 1979.

SKERNE Wesleyan 1839 former school, cl., ho., rec. 1986.

SKIDBY (1) Baptist 1819, cl. c. 1877, der. 1892, dem.
(2) Wesleyan 1820, cl. 1902, village hall, rec. 1987.
(3) Wesleyan 1902, arch. Gelder & Kitchen, in use, rec. 1987.

SKIPSEA (1) Independent (Congregational) 1801, reb. 1875, arch. J. Stork, dem. **(2) Quaker**, late 17th cent., fell down by 1779. **(3) Wesleyan** 1800, reb. 1836 and 1910, arch. attrib. S. Dyer, in use, rec. 1989. **(4) Primitive** 1845, cl., reading room, rec. 1989.

SKIPWITH Primitive 1868-9, in use, rec. 1989.

SKIRLAUGH (1) Wesleyan 1821, cl. 1893, dem.
(2) Wesleyan 1893, cl. c. 1973, shop, rec. 1989.
(3) Primitive 1821, cl. 1859, reading room, dem.
(4) Primitive 1859, dem.

SLEDMERE (1) Wesleyan 1889, dem. **(2) Primitive** 1889, arch. attrib. W. Petch, Middleton, in use, rec. 1988.

SOUTH CAVE (1) Independent (Congregational), lic. 1718, repl. 1873, arch. S. Musgrave, in use (URC), rec. 1988. **(2) Wesleyan** 1816, cl. 1943, garage, rec. 1988.
(3) Primitive 1837, reb. 1876-7, arch. W. Freeman, in use, rec. 1988.

SOUTH DALTON Wesleyan 1825, cl. c. 1961, ho., rec. 1988.

SOUTH DUFFIELD Wesleyan 1824, cl. 1969, store, rec. 1989.

Stamford Bridge Wesleyan chapel, 1828.

SOUTHBURN Wesleyan 1848, cl. 1963, dem.

SPALDINGTON Wesleyan 1788, reb. 1820, cl. by 1870s, became school 1877, rec. 1988.

SPEETON Wesleyan 1847, reb. 1925.

SPROATLEY Wesleyan 1804, rest. 1904, in use, rec. 1980.

STAMFORD BRIDGE (1) Wesleyan 1796, cl. 1828, ho., r. 1979. **(2) Wesleyan** 1828, in use, rec. 1989. **(3) Primitive** 1866, cl. by 1935, store, rec. 1989.

STAXTON (1) Wesleyan 1813, cl., dem. after 1971.
(2) Primitive 1847, in use, rec. 1988.

STILLINGFLEET Wesleyan 1819, in use, rec. 1989.

STORWOOD (1) Wesleyan 1837, cl. 1895, dem.
(2) Wesleyan 1895, cl. by 1954, dem.

SUNK ISLAND Wesleyan 1847, reb. 1858, cl. 1956, dem. c.1968.

SUTTON UPON DERWENT (1) **Wesleyan** 1838, in use 1851, cl. by 1865. (2) **Wesleyan** 1882, corrugated iron, cl. in 1920s, dem. (3) **Primitive**, registered 1861, deregistered 1876.

SUTTON-ON-HULL (1) **Wesleyan**, Church St., c. 1812, cl. 1859, now possibly part of recreation club, rec., 1987. (2) **Wesleyan**, Church St., 1959, in use, rec. 1987. (3) **Primitive**, Chamberlain St., 1832, reb. 1855, cl. 1876, dem. (4) **Primitive**, College St., 1876, arch. J. Wright, cl. 1933, hall, rec. 1987.

SWANLAND (1) **Independent (Congregational)** 1693, reb. 1803, schools added 1877, in use (URC/Methodist), rec. 1987. (2) **Primitive** 1828, cl., store, rec. 1987.

SWINE (1) **Wesleyan** 1829, cl. 1893, dem. (2) **Wesleyan** 1893, cl., ho., rec. 1989.

THEARNE Primitive 1828, reb. 1867, cl. 1958, offices, rec. 1987.

THIXENDALE Wesleyan 1837, rest. 1906, arch. J. Butterworth, Pocklington, cl. 1974, store, rec. 1987.

THORGANBY Wesleyan 1815, reb. 1861 and 1909, in use, rec. 1989.

THORNGUMBALD (1) **Independent/Methodist** 1800, became solely Independent (Congregational) then taken over by **Primitives** by 1879, cl. 1936, village hall then farm buildings, largely dem. 1970s. (2) **Wesleyan**, 1840, reb. 1904, in use, rec. 1981.

THORNHOLME Primitive 1892, cl., dem. 1986, rec. 1977.

THORNTON Wesleyan 1909, arch. T. Monkman, York, cl. 1974, store, rec.

THORPE BASSETT Wesleyan 1844, dem.

Tickton Wesleyan chapel, 1877.

Ulrome Wesleyan chapel, 1905.

THWING (1) **Wesleyan** 1815, reb. 1839 and 1906, cl. 1970s, ho., rec. 1989. (2) **Primitive** 1840, cl., dem. after 1937.

TIBTHORPE Wesleyan 1823, enl. 1850, rest. and enl. 1905, cl. 1969, dem. 1970s.

TICKTON (1) **Wesleyan** 1828, cl. 1877, office, rec. 1987. (2) **Wesleyan** 1877, in use, rec. 1989.

ULROME (1) **Wesleyan** 1848, cl. 1905, garage, rec. 1987. (2) **Wesleyan** 1905, in use, rec. 1987.

UNCLEBY Wesleyan 1796, cl. 1974, workshop, rec. 1984.

WALKINGTON (1) **Wesleyan** 1822, enl. 1869, cl. 1887, Sunday school then farm building, rec. 1988.
(2) **Wesleyan** 1887, arch. A. Gelder, alt. 1962, arch. Bernard Blanchard, in use, r. 1988. (3) **Primitive** 1837, Northgate, cl. 1879, ho., rec. 1988. (4) **Primitive** 1879, dem. 1962.

WANSFORD (1) **Wesleyan** 1809, cl. 1963. (2) **Primitive** 1864, cl. 1906, village hall, rec. 1989.

WARTER (1) **Wesleyan** 1808, rest. 1839, reb. 1878, cl. 1974, ho., rec. 1987. (2) **Primitive** by 1892, dem.

WATTON Primitive 1887, arch. attrib. W. Petch, Middleton, cl. 1969, ho., rec. 1986.

WAWNE Primitive 1860, enl., in use, rec. 1989.

WEAVERTHORPE (1) **Wesleyan** 1794, reb. 1814?, alt. 1914, in use, rec. 1984. (2) **Primitive** 1841, rest. 1888, dem.

WEEL Primitive 1860, cl. 1963, store, rec. 1989.

WELTON (1) **Unitarian** c.1850, dem. (2) **Wesleyan** 1815, dem. (3) **Primitive** 1869, dem.

WELWICK (1) **Quaker**, Humber Lane, 1718, cl. 1818,

Wansford Primitive Methodist chapel, 1865.

school in 1850s, ho. from c. 1910, rec. 1980. (2) **Wesleyan** 1849, cl. c. 1932, burnt down 1945. (3) **Primitive** 1848, cl. 1911, dem. (4) **Primitive** 1911, in use, rec. 1980.

WEST ELLA Wesleyan, by 1856, reb. 1895, in use, rec. 1987.

WEST HESLERTON Wesleyan 1839, cl., ho., rec. 1984.

WESTOW (1) **Wesleyan** 1793, cl. 1906, workshop, rec. 1984. (2) **Wesleyan** 1906, arch. A. Barnes, Malton, in use, rec. 1989. (3) **Primitive** 1873, dem.

WETWANG (1) **Wesleyan** 1812, cl. 1886, Sunday school until 1963, shop, rec. 1986. (2) **Wesleyan** 1886, arch. J. Earnshaw, cl. 1963, dem. 1978. (3) **Primitive** 1824, reb. 1869, cl. 1959, dem. 1961.

WHELDRAKE Wesleyan 1816, reb. 1863, enl. 1894, cl. 1970, ho., rec. 1984.

WILBERFOSS (1) **Wesleyan** 1841, enl. 1905-6, cl. 1974, ho., rec. 1989. (2) **Primitive** 1824, reb. 1872, cl. 1937, ho., rec. 1989.

WILLERBY (Kirk Ella) (1) **Primitive** 1850, cl. 1897, workshop, rec. 1987. (2) **Primitive** 1897, schoolroom added 1900, cl. 1965, Methodist hall, rec. 1987.

WILLITOFT Wesleyan 1894, cl., store and garage, rec. 1977.

WINTRINGHAM Wesleyan 1834, cl., garage, rec. 1984.

WITHERNSEA (1) **Congregational**, Queen St., 1903, arch. W. H. Bingley, in use (URC), rec. 1989.
(2) **Wesleyan** Northgate (Owthorne), 1804, cl. 1857, ho., rec. 1989. (3) **Wesleyan**, Cammidge St., 1857, cl. 1900, dem. (4) **Wesleyan**, Queen St., 1900-1, arch. Gelder & Kitchen, cl. 1962, dem. (5) **Primitive**, Alma St., 1858, cl. 1878, garage, rec. 1989. (6) **Primitive**, Hull Rd., 1878-9, arch. W. Freeman, in use, rec. 1989.

WITHERNWICK (1) **Wesleyan** 1810, Sunday school 1845, chap. reb. 1914, in use, rec. 1987. (2) **Primitive** 1843, cl., garage, rec. 1987.

WOLD NEWTON (1) **Wesleyan** 1839, cl. c. 1980, hall, rec. 1989. (2) **Primitive** 1841, reb. 1870, cl., dem.

WOODMANSEY (1) **Particular Baptist**, King St., 1872, cl. c. 1940, dem. (2) **Church Methodist**, King St., 1825, cl., dem.

WYTON Wesleyan 1841, in use, rec. 1980.

YAPHAM Wesleyan 1865, enl. 1953, cl. 1974, ho., rec. 1989

YEDDINGHAM Wesleyan 1842, cl.

YOKEFLEET Wesleyan by 1856, replaced by corrugated iron building, rec. 1977.

Wyton Wesleyan chapel, 1841.

APPENDIX B: CHAPEL ARCHITECTS

Much of the information on Hull architects has been kindly supplied by Chris Ketchell.

ATKINSON, T. Beecroft (fl. 1900-35) of Hull. Architect of Primitive Methodist chapels at Patrington Haven (1905), Keyingham (1909), and Hessle (1909). Alderman of Hull.

BARNES, Alfred of Malton. Architect and builder, designed Westow Wesleyan chapel (1906).

BENNISON, Appleton (1750-1830) of Hull. Mason and architect, responsible for Cottingham Zion Congregational chapel (1819).

BINGLEY, W. H. (fl. 1890-1907) of Hull. Architect of Withernsea Congregational chapel (1903). Other works include Newland Orphan Homes, Cottingham Rd., Hull (1892), Fish Street Memorial Congregational church, Princes Ave., Hull (1899), Boulevard Free Methodist church, Hull (1907). Pupil or partner of Samuel Musgrave (see below).

BOTTERILL, William (1820-1903) of Hull. An active Wesleyan, he designed many Wesleyan chapels including the early Gothic chapel at Newland (1857-8) and impressive chapels at Market Weighton (1868), Bridlington Quay (1873), and Hessle (1876). He designed at least three Wesleyan chapels in Hull and others at Market Rasen (1863), Alford (1864), and Barnetby (1879) in Lincolnshire. Botterill was established as an architect and surveyor in Hull by 1851. He worked for the York & North Midland Railway in 1852-3 and Hull School Board from 1873. He designed many houses, banks, offices and industrial buildings in Hull from 1852 and was responsible for the laying out of the Newland Park Estate in 1877. His pupil John Bilson (1853-1943), the celebrated architectural historian, took over the partnership in 1899 as Botterill Son & Bilson.

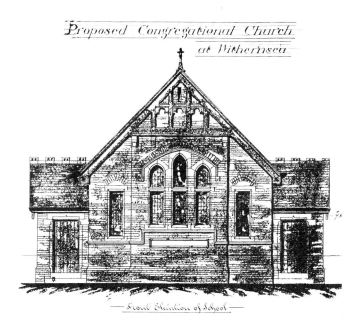

Withernsea Congregational church. Elevation of school by W. H. Bingley, 1903. (Humberside County Archives Office)

BUTTERWORTH, Joseph of Pocklington. Architect for restoration of Wesleyan chapels at Thixendale (1906) and Acklam (1909).

CHANNON, C. H. of Malton. Architect of Settrington Wesleyan chapel (1890). Partner of John Gibson of Malton (see below) from 1882.

DANBY, George Francis (b.1845) of Leeds. Architect for Pocklington Wesleyan Circuit, being responsible for new chapels at Catton (1899), Seaton Ross (1900), Millington (1900), and Newton on Derwent (1901), and restoration and alterations at Elvington (1899), Melbourne (1899), and Bishop Wilton (1900). Danby set up practice in Leeds in 1872 and designed villas in Roundhay and Headingley. He also specialised in Wesleyan chapels and schools, designing several in Leeds in 1874-1906 and others in Shipley and Middlesbrough.

DYER, Samuel of Bridlington. Architect of the distinctive Wesleyan chapel at Bempton (1903) and possibly the chapels at Kilham (1907) and Skipsea (1910). Dyer was in practice at Bridlington Quay by 1892.

Bempton Wesleyan chapel, by Samuel Dyer, 1903.

Skipsea Wesleyan chapel, attributed to Samuel Dyer, 1910.

EARNSHAW, Joseph (c. 1845-1914) of Bridlington. An active member of the Bridlington Quay Wesleyan chapel and manager of the Wesleyan day school. Architect of numerous chapels, the first seemingly being Bridlington United Methodist Free Church chapel on the Promenade (1872) (now demolished). For this chapel he did all the decorative plasterwork at home in the evening as his personal contribution. Other known chapels by Earnshaw are Bridlington Quay Trinity Congregational chapel (1879), and Wesleyan chapels at Foston (1879), Rudston (1879), Bridlington (Burlington, St. John St. 1884), Wetwang (1886 dem.) and possibly Flamborough (1889 dem.). The Salvation Army Citadel, Wellington Rd., Bridlington was also by Earnshaw, being originally built as a temperance hall (1876-7).

Foston Wesleyan chapel, by Joseph Earnshaw, 1879.

Earnshaw was born at Heanor, Derbyshire, the son of a builder. Moved from Sheffield to Bridlington in 1869 to supervise the building of Marlborough Terrace and the Crescent for G. W. Travis, formerly of Sheffield. He became the foremost architect/surveyor of Victorian Bridlington, being closely involved with most of the large-scale housing developments.

FIPPARD, Herbert of York. Architect of Middleton on the Wolds Primitive chapel (1864) and for the alterations to Driffield Primitive chapel (1865). Also designed Selby Primitive chapel (1862).

Withernsea Primitive Methodist chapel, by William Freeman, 1879.

FREEMAN, William (fl. 1872-86) of Hull. A prolific chapel architect with a distinctive style. He designed Primitive Methodist chapels at Halsham (1873), South Cave (1876), Bridlington (St. John's, 1877), North Newbald (1878), Withernsea (1878-9), Bridlington (Central, 1879), Hull (Lincoln St., 1872; Beecroft St., 1873), and Goole (1875). Architect of numerous houses and offices in Hull.

GELDER, Sir (William) Alfred (1855-1941) of Hull. An active Wesleyan, he served as a local preacher, Sunday school teacher and circuit steward. He was the architect of many local Wesleyan chapels in the late 19th and early 20th centuries, including the following in the East Riding: Walkington (1877), Eastrington (1893), Withernsea (1900-1, Gelder & Kitchen), and Skidby (1902).

Gelder, the son of a North Cave farmer, was apprenticed to the architects Robert Clamp of Hull and W. H. Harris of Leeds. Commenced practice in Hull in 1877. The Wesleyan mission chapel at Barton upon Humber (1882) is his earliest recorded chapel. Other major chapels by Gelder or the partnership of Gelder & Kitchen included, in Hull, Lambert St. Primitive (1893-4 with T. B. Thompson), Argyle St. Wesleyan (1894), Newland Ave. Wesleyan school/chapel (1901), Bethesda Primitive, Holland St. (1902), Queens Hall, Wesleyan mission hall, Alfred Gelder St. (1903-5), Princes Ave. Wesleyan Methodist church, Hull (1905), Portobello St. Primitive (1906), and Newland Methodist church, Cottingham Rd. (1927-8). The firm also designed Legsby Ave. Methodist church, Grimsby (1909). Gelder, a Liberal councillor in Hull, five times Mayor (1899-1903), was M.P. for the Brigg division in 1910-18. He was knighted in 1903. Responsible for many major buildings in Hull and the Edwardian replanning of the city centre.

GIBSON, John (1811-87) of Malton. Nonconformist, initially a Baptist but joined Congregational church in 1863 and became a deacon. Architect of Norton Primitive Methodist chapel (1864). Builder and architect at Scarborough from 1841, where he laid out the Southcliff development. Moved to Malton by 1847 and was the leading architect of mid-Victorian Malton and Norton. In 1882 he took C. H. Channon (see above) into partnership.

GRANT, Thomas (1823-1907) of Pocklington. Builder and architect. He designed the Wesleyan school (1852) and a circuit minister's house (1869) in Chapmangate, Pocklington, and Wesleyan chapels at Leppington (1867), Barmby Moor (1869), Allerthorpe (1869), and Bolton (1869). On his death Grant was said to have been the builder of 'the major part of the principal property in Pocklington'.

HAWE, William (1822-97) of Beverley and Driffield. A highly prolific architect responsible for many houses and commercial and industrial buildings in Beverley, Driffield, Market Weighton and district. His earliest recorded works were Driffield Baptist chapel and Hutton Cranswick Wesleyan chapel (both 1861). He was also responsible for alterations to Gt. Driffield Wesleyan chapel in 1862. He later took his stepson J. R. Foley into partnership and Hawe & Foley designed the Scotch Baptist chapel in Wilbert Lane, Beverley (1888).

IBBOTSON, H. of Pocklington. Architect of Pocklington Primitive Methodist chapel (1820).

JOBSON, Frederick James (1812-81). Born Northwich; moved to Lincoln, where he was apprenticed to Edward James Willson, Roman Catholic architect and antiquarian. Entered Wesleyan ministry and appointed to Patrington Circuit in 1834. On three occasions he served for a three years' term at the City Road Chapel, London. He was President of Wesleyan Methodist Conference in 1869. With the sponsorship of the Wesleyan Chapel Committee he published *Chapel and School Architecture* in 1850. This work which strongly advocated the use of the Gothic style, had a major influence on Wesleyan chapel architecture. The design of the Wesleyan chapel at Duggleby (1856) was said to have been taken directly from Jobson's book.

JOHNSON, William of Howden. Architect of Kilpin Wesleyan chapel (1867). Other local works include Rawcliffe Board School (1878).

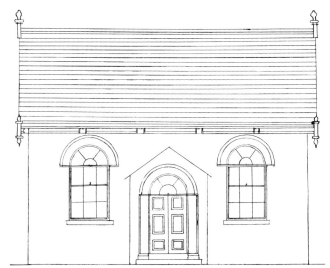

Allerthorpe. Elevation of Wesleyan chapel, by Thomas Grant, 1869. (Humberside County Archives Office).

LOVEL, William of Norton. Builder and timber merchant. Architect of Norton Wesleyan chapel (1857).

MONKMAN, Thomas of York. Architect of Thornton Wesleyan chapel (1909).

MORLEY, W. J., (Morley & Woodhouse) of Bradford. Architect of Beverley Wesleyan chapel, Toll Gavel (1890-2) and adjoining schoolroom (1903). Other chapels by Morley include Groves chapel, York (1833), and the octagonal Eastbrook Hall, Bradford (1903).

MUSGRAVE, Samuel (fl. 1870-85) of Hull. A High Church Anglican who was architect of numerous nonconformist chapels as well as Anglican churches. Designed Hornsea Congregational church (1872), S. Cave Congregational church (1873), Bridlington Baptist chapel (1874), and Elloughton Congregational church (1876), and was responsible for the alterations, refronting and schoolroom at Pocklington Congregational church (1878). Amongst his other works were board schools and houses in Hull as well as St. Silas's church (1870), St.

Barnabas's church, Hessle Rd. (1873), Latimer Congregational church, Williamson St. (1874), Hessle Road Congregational church (1877), Brunswick Methodist church, Holderness Rd. (1877), and Queens Road Wesleyan chapel (1878), all in Hull, and the Corn Exchange and Baths, Beverley (1885).

NOBLE, A. J. Primitive Methodist minister and architect of Rudston Primitive Methodist chapel (1877).

PAULL, Henry John (d.1888) of Manchester. The favourite architect of the dominant nonconformist community of Driffield, where he designed the Congregational church (1863) both in Exchange St., as well as the private house Millfield (1865-6), (a forerunner of Highfield) for the Congregationalist shopkeeper Henry Angas. The success of these commissions led him to be employed later as architect for Driffield board school (1873-4) and the massive Wesleyan chapel (1880).

Paull's introduction to Driffield would have come through his work for John Crossley of Halifax, the Congregationalist carpet manufacturer, for whom he designed, with his partner Ayliffe, West Hill Park estate, Halifax (1863-8). Paull was the architect of several Congregational churches including, in London, the important Christ Church chapel, Westminster Bridge Rd. (1872, with Bickerdike), and Islington Congregational chapel, Upper St. (1888, with Bonella).

PENNINGTON, George F. of Garside and Pennington. Architect of Beverley Particular Baptist chapel (1909-10).

PETCH, William (1826-1919) of Middleton on the Wolds. A wheelwright 'who, as builder and architect, has done much to improve our Wolds chapels' (H. Woodcock, *Piety amongst the Peasantry*, 1889, p. 121). Petch was born at Goodmanham, apprenticed to Richard Vary at Lund by 1841, and married Vary's daughter. Moved to Middleton in 1857 where he became

Great Driffield *Congregational church, by H. J. Paull, 1866.*

the leading figure in the Primitive Methodist chapel. He was chapel steward, trustee, class leader and local preacher from 1859. He designed Primitive Methodist chapels at Lockington (1862) and Little Driffield (1878). The following can also be attributed to him: Wansford (1864), Lund (1871), Watton (1887), Beswick (1888), and Sledmere (1889).

PETCH, J. Caleb of Scarborough. Architect of Norwood Primitive Methodist chapel, Beverley (1901).

Coniston Primitive Methodist chapel.

PETTINGELL, Frank Noble (1848-83) of Hull. Architect and water colour artist. Designed Primitive Methodist chapels at Coniston (1872), Hedon (1873), and Williamson St., Hull (1873). Drew bird's eye view of Hull c.1880.

PRATT, T. of Bubwith. A builder who was architect of Primitive Methodist chapels at Riccall (1857) and Bubwith (1862).

RANGER, William of London. Leading Wesleyan architect who designed chapels at Langtoft (1874), Cottingham (1878-9), and Nunburnholme (1879).

Nunburnholme Wesleyan chapel, by William Ranger, 1879.

SHARP, of York (possibly Richard Hey Sharp fl. 1820-50). Architect of Howden Congregational chapel (1837).

SHAW Brothers of Howden. Designed new front for Howden Congregational chapel (1878).

SHEPHERDSON, John Frank of Driffield. Architect of Lockington Wesleyan chapel (1874), alterations to North Frodingham Congregational chapel (1878), and the new front for Driffield Baptist chapel (1884).

SHEPHERDSON, Joseph. Architect of Bridlington Congregational church (1906).

SHERWOOD, E. J. of London. Architect of Salvation Army Citadel, Beverley (1885).

SMITHSON, W. C. of Leeds. Architect of Primitive Methodist chapels at Market Weighton (1902) and Barmby Marsh (1902).

SMITH, Richard George (fl. 1861-98) of Hull. The earliest known work of this important Hull architect is the modest Wesleyan chapel at Grindale (1861). By 1875 Smith was in partnership with Frederick Stead Brodrick. Smith and Smith & Broderick were architects of numerous major buildings in Hull and the East Riding, including the Anglican churches of Holy Trinity, Bridlington (1871), and St. Nicholas, Grindale (1875), De la Pole Hospital, Willerby (1883), Northumberland Avenue Almshouses, Hull, (1887), East Riding County Hall, Beverley (1890), and St. John of Beverley Catholic church, Beverley (1897-8).

STORK, J. Architect of Skipsea Congregational chapel (1875).

SULMAN, John (1849-1934) of London. Architect of Market Weighton Congregational church (1881). Sulman, later Sir John, worked in London from 1870 to

1885, then went to Australia where be became a leading architect and town planner. He designed several Congregational churches, including the church and schools, Highbury Quadrant, London (1880-2).

TAYLOR, Charles E. Architect of Driffield United Methodist Free Church chapel (1863).

TAYLOR, Edward of York. Architect of Pocklington Wesleyan chapel (1864) and the similar Wesleyan chapel at Snaith. In York Taylor designed the City Art Gallery (1879) and Wesleyan chapels in Melbourne St. (1877) and at Heworth (1890) and Clifton (1909).

THOMPSON, Thomas Brownlow (d.1929) of Hull. An officer of the Presbyterian church. Architect of Beverley Congregational church (1886-7) and Burstwick Primitive Methodist chapel (1898). Established in Hull by 1876, possibly in association with F. N. Pettingell (see above), Thompson was responsible for many other nonconformist buildings in the area, including Wesleyan chapel, St. Georges Rd., Hull (1877), Wesleyan chapel, Belton, Lincs. (1878), St. Columba's Presbyterian church, Priory St., York (1879), Presbyterian church, New Clee, Lincs. (1881), Primitive Methodist chapel, Goxhill, Lincs. (1891), Primitive Methodist chapel, Lambert St., Hull (1893-4 with Alfred Gelder), Presbyterian church, Anlaby Rd., Hull (1893), Primitive Methodist chapel, Selby St., Hull (1901), and the Boulevard Baptist church, Hull (1903, in partnership with John F. Fisher). Firm became T. Brownlow Thompson and Fisher, then Fisher Hollingsworth.

TRUELOVE, George. Architect of Bridlington Wesleyan Reform chapel (1852).

WEBSTER, J. T. of Hedon. Architect of Hedon Wesleyan chapel (1875).

Pocklington Wesleyan Methodist chapel, by Edward Taylor, 1864. *(Drawing by Eugene Fisk)*

WRIGHT, Joseph (1818-1885) of Hull. Wright, an active Primitive Methodist, was the great architect of the Connexion being responsible for numerous chapels in Hull, East Yorkshire and North Lincolnshire during 20 years from the late 1850s. Seventeen East Riding Primitive chapels are known to have been designed by Joseph Wright or can be attributed to him: Hessle (1857), Nafferton (1858), Cottingham (1861), Patrington (1862), Hornsea (1864), Preston (1867), Beverley (1868), Roos (1868), Hotham (1869), North Cave (1870), Bridlington (1870), Filey (1870), Garton on the Wolds (1871), Gt. Driffield (1873), Beeford (1873), Flamborough (1874) and Sutton-on-Hull (1876). In Hull Wright designed chapels in Holderness Rd. (1862), Bright St. (1863), Spring Bank (1864), Anlaby Rd. (Bourne Chapel 1871), and Fountain Rd. (1877). Elsewhere in Yorkshire there were chapels by Wright at Tadcaster (1864) and Scarborough (1865), and in Lincolnshire he was responsible for chapels at Barton, Cleethorpes, Grimsby, Market Rasen (1866), South Ferriby (1864), and Winterton (1868-9). Wright was a pupil of Cuthbert Brodrick.

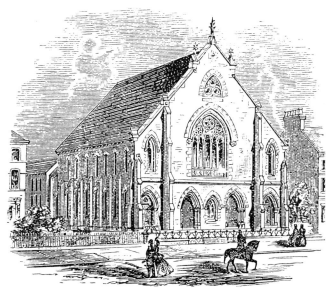

Nafferton Primitive Methodist chapel, by Joseph Wright, 1858. Demolished.

Joseph Wright.

Hull: Bourne Chapel, Anlaby Road, 1871. A rare Gothic building by Joseph Wright. Demolished.

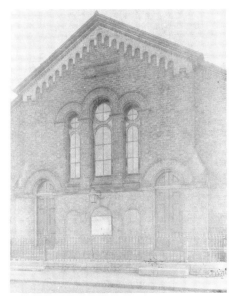

North Cave *Primitive Methodist chapel, by Joseph Wright, 1870. (Postcard C. Ketchell)*

Great Driffield *Primitive Methodist chapel, by Joseph Wright, 1873. Front demolished. (Postcard C. Ketchell)*

Sutton-on-Hull *Primitive Methodist chapel, attributed to Joseph Wright, 1876.*

Hornsea *Primitive Methodist chapel, by Joseph Wright, 1864.*

SOURCES

For a general account of sources for East Riding nonconformity see David Neave, 'Post-Reformation Religion', in B. Dyson, ed., *A Guide to Local Studies in East Yorkshire*, Cherry Burton, 1985, pp. 75-88.

Original records of nonconformity in Humberside County Archives Office and the Borthwick Institute of Historical Research, York, have been a major source for this study. Chapel and meeting house dates are obtainable from a variety of sources relating to the registration of dissenters' meeting houses under the Toleration Act of 1689 and from the religious census returns of 1851 and local trade directories. Information on architects has been chiefly obtained from newspaper reports, entries in the *Wesleyan Methodist Magazine* and *Primitive Methodist Magazine*, and original circuit and chapel records in Humberside County Archives Office.

The volumes of the *Victoria County History, East Riding*, have as always proved invaluable. Chapels were located by using the first and later editions of the 6 inch to the mile Ordnance Survey maps.

NONCONFORMIST ARCHITECTURE

Barton, D. A., *Discovering Chapels and Meeting Houses*, Princes Risborough, 1975.

Blanchard, B. W., 'Nonconformist churches in the Hull district', unpublished dissertation, Hull School of Architecture, 1955 (copy in Hull Local History Library).

Briggs, M. S., *Puritan Architecture and its future*, London, 1946.

Clapham, J. A., *Gothic Congregational Churches*, London, 1904.

Council for British Archaeology, *Hallelujah! Recording chapels and meeting houses*, London, 1985.

Dolbey, G. W., *The Architectural Expression of Methodism : The First Hundred Years*, London, 1964.

Hague, G and J., *The Unitarian Heritage : An Architectural Survey of Chapels and Churches in the Unitarian tradition in the British Isles,* Sheffield, 1986.

Jobson, F. J., *Chapel and School Architecture*, London, 1850.

Jones, A., *Welsh Chapels*, Cardiff, 1984.

Jones, R. P., *Nonconformist church architecture*, London 1914.

Lindley, K., *Chapels and Meeting Houses*, London, 1969.

Powell, K., *The Fall of Zion : Northern chapel architecture and its future*, London, 1980.

Stell, C. F., *Nonconformist Chapels and Meeting-Houses in Central England*, London, 1986.

Willis, R., *Nonconformist Chapels of York 1693-1840*, York, n.d.

EAST YORKSHIRE NONCONFORMITY

Dale, B. *Yorkshire Puritanism and Early Nonconformity*, Bradford, 1910.

Darwent, C. E., *Story of Fish Street Church, Hull*, Hull, 1898 (Independent/Congregational church in Hull and East Riding).

Kendall, H. B., *The Origin and History of the Primitive Methodist Church*, 2 vols., London, c. 1906.

Lyth, J., *Glimpses of Early Methodism in York and the Surrounding District*, York, 1885.

Miall, J. G. *Congregationalism in Yorkshire*, London, 1868.

Rushton, J. H. *They Kept Faith : The History of some Yorkshire Christian Congregations*, Pickering, 1967.

Thistlethwaite, W. P., *The Quaker Meeting Houses of*

Yorkshire 1647-1980, Harrogate, 1982, additions 1985.

Thistlethwaite, W. P., *Yorkshire Quarterly Meeting 1665-1966*, Harrogate, 1979 (Society of Friends).

Woodcock, H., *Piety among the Peasantry, being sketches of Primitive Methodism on the Yorkshire Wolds*, London, 1889.

Yorkshire Baptist Association, *Baptists of Yorkshire : centenary memorial volume*, 1912.

LOCAL STUDIES

There are many studies of individual chapels and congregations, the majority being produced for centenary or other celebrations. The Yorkshire Branch of the Wesley Historical Society has a considerable number in its archives at Yorkshire Archaeological Society, Claremont, Leeds. Below is a selection of those found most useful in compiling this booklet.

Baker, F., *The Story of Methodism in Newland*, Hull, 1958.

Brown, H. F., *The Story of Methodism in Hessle 1820-1977*, Hessle, 1977.

East, J. T., *Souvenir of the Centenary of the Driffield Circuit*, Driffield, 1909.

Morris, H. K., *The Methodist Chapels of Burstwick in Holderness: a short history and description*, Burstwick, 1979.

Richardson, C. B., *Methodism in Hedon*, Hedon, 1973.

Rigby, P., ed. *A Cottingham Century. A Scrapbook Celebrating the Centenary of Hallgate Methodist Church, Cottingham, 1878-1978*, Cottingham, 1978.

Scrowston, R. M., *A Hundred Years of Methodism in Walkington*, Walkington, 1987.

Skingle, E. H., *The Story of a Country Baptist Church, Bishop Burton, East Yorkshire*, Hull, 1929.

Smith, E. B., *Zion United Reformed Church, Cottingham*, Cottingham, 1982.

Solomon, C. J., *The Pocklington Methodist Circuit 1786-1986: a bi-centenary history*, Pocklington, 1986.

Verity, H., *Founded on the Rock. An account of Primitive Methodism in Withernsea and district and the Hull Road Chapel 1879-1979*, Withernsea, 1979.

Withernsea Primitive Methodist chapel, Hull Road, 1879.

ACKNOWLEDGEMENTS

We are indebted to many people for assistance with the survey of nonconformist buildings, and in particular Keith Allison, Rod Ambler, Geoff Bell, the late Philip Brown, Margaret Bryan, Norman Creaser, Graham Kent, Margery Matthews, Brian Precious, E. C. Robson, Rex Russell, P. Thompson, and Richard Walgate. Special thanks are due to Eugene Fisk who made drawings of chapels for this publication, and to Chris Ketchell for information on architects and for allowing us to reproduce a number of postcards from his collection. Permission to reproduce chapel and circuit plans was granted by Humberside County Archives Office and the relevant Methodist Circuit.

We are most grateful for the assistance given by Keith Holt, Carol Boddington, Bob Hale and all the staff at Humberside County Archives Office, the staff at Hull Local History Library and Beverley Reference Library, and the staff of the Borthwick Institute of Historical Research, York.

The Yorkshire Archaeological Society Grants Fund generously provided financial assistance.

In 1988 a Chapels Society was founded for the promotion of public knowledge of the architectural and historical importance of chapels, meeting houses, and other non-Anglican places of worship. All interested in chapels are urged to join this society and help ensure a future for this most important, yet threatened, aspect of life and landscape of our country. Details of membership are obtainable from Christopher Stell, Hon,. Secretary, The Chapels Society, Frognal, 25 Berks Hill, Chorleywood, Herts., WD3 5AG

Howden Wesleyan Methodist chapel during demolition, 1974.

Hutton Cranswick *Primitive Methodist chapel, 1864, in process of demolition, 1970.*